TAMING PERSONAL DEBT

PAUL SAMPSON

McGraw-Hill Ryerson Limited

Toronto   Montréal   New York   Auckland   Bogotá
Caracas   Lisbon   London   Madrid   Mexico   Milan
New Delhi   San Juan   Singapore   Sydney   Tokyo

ISBN: 0-07-552922-X

1 2 3 4 5 6 7 8 9 0   B B M   6 5 4 3 2 1 0 9 8 7

Printed and bound in Canada

Canadian Cataloguing in Publication

Sampson, Paul, 1960-
    Taming personal debt
Includes index

ISBN 0-07-522922-X

1. Debt.   2. Finance, personal.   I. Title.

HG179.S35 1997   332.024'02   C97-930697-3

Publisher: *Joan Homewood*
Editor: *Erin Moore*
Production Coordinator: *Jennifer Burnell*
Editorial Services: *Rachel Mansfield*
Cover Design: *Sharon Matthews*
Interior Design/Composition: *Lynda Powell*
Printer: *Best Book Manufacturers*
Typefaces: *Linotype Centennial and ITC Kabel*

To
my wife Nancy
and our children,
Gerry, Jessica and Sarah

■ ■ ■ ■

Acknowledgements

I would like to thank all those who helped make this book possible. In particular: Nancy Sampson, my wife, for working with me every step of the way, and along with my children for making personal sacrifices while I worked on this project; Gerry Sampson, my father, who always provided sound financial advice; my brothers Mark and Peter Sampson, for their input and support; Dan Sullivan, my business partner for over ten years; Joan Homewood, my publisher, and the rest of the staff at McGraw-Hill Ryerson who worked on this project, Suzanne Tobin, Erin Moore, and Rachel Mansfield, for their expertise, advice, support and patience.

Contents

Introduction

Congratulations, you have made a wise decision by purchasing this book. Debt problems generally are a result of a lack of information rather than a lack of money, so my objective is to have you well informed when you finish reading this book. I know it will inspire you to become debt free and help you use financing to your advantage. We live in a world where it is virtually impossible to live without credit if we aspire to own expensive things such as a home. However, credit is misused every day and it can limit our ability to own the things which credit was supposed to help us acquire. Credit was designed as a vehicle that would allow you to purchase, for example, a house, which would be next to impossible to save for otherwise.

By purchasing this book it is safe to assume that you have some level of debt. I personally do not know how good or bad your particular situation may be at this time, but because we will be covering several different aspects of credit use, this book will help you make educated decisions throughout your lifetime.

This book will guide you to do the following:

- [$] Identify the warning signs of a possible financial crisis;
- [$] Pay off your debt in the most effective way;
- [$] Determine the most appropriate uses of credit;
- [$] Find out where all your money goes;
- [$] Save over $100,000 dollars in interest payments over your lifetime;
- [$] Deal with creditors and lawyers;

$ Maximize profits in your small business;

$ Determine some financial goals for yourself.

The book was designed to be straight to the point and easy to read. You can read it cover to cover or go directly to the areas which concern you most, but I advise you to eventually read the entire book. There are easy to understand examples following the more difficult strategies. There are worksheets to help you get organized.

My Own Story

I was inspired to write this book by a radio talk program I was listening to while driving my car in July 1993. The program was about young adults and the difficulties facing them, such as the unstable employment situation that was affecting their financial stability. While I was listening a flood of memories started coming back to me of a time when I was in a severe financial crisis. Though I was only in my early thirties at the time, I had already experienced the problems they were having and I remember thinking that someone should write a book to educate people on how to manage their finances. I knew there were several books available on how to invest your money but if you can't pay your bills they aren't of much use to you. I also knew there was almost nothing available to the public regarding how to manage debt or how to get out of debt. The reason I knew this was because I would have read it. I had been obsessed with this very topic for the past six or seven years and was always looking for anything that would help my situation.

So, since no one else has done it, I decided I would write this book based on my personal experiences along with my research. The first thing my research proved was that this was not a problem limited to young adults. My research also proves that debt problems as well as solutions are not affected by age. You have heard all the buzz words, rightsizing, downsizing, streamlining, mergers, acquisitions, corporate takeovers. Many people are now faced with the possibility of losing their job or have become unemployed for the first time in their lives, forcing them to rethink their personal financial situations.

I started establishing credit in my teens with car loans and by the age of twenty-two I qualified for a mortgage, although I waited until I was twenty-four before I actually purchased a house. When I was twenty-five I started my own business. I had no income so I used my credit cards for my living expenses for about a year until we started taking a paycheck. I had two partners and things were going along reasonably well until we started to borrow money for the expansion of the business.

Our financial deterioration was the result of a series of problems that occurred over a short period of time, combined with the fact that our business had experienced rapid growth, and we were inexperienced managers. The rapid growth forced us to use most of our profits to expand our business. When the stock market crashed in October 1987 our account base consisted of a large number of small companies on the stock exchange that stopped using our services. We also had one of our largest customers go into receivership, and since we were an unsecured creditor we were unable to collect any money from them. Very early in 1988 many of the small companies to whom we provided services had folded and we were unable to collect any money from them. So in a matter of months we went from increased sales to decreased sales, had lost about $40,000 to bad debts and added a tax bill for profits we never collected. The bank called our loan; we had collection agencies calling our office hourly. When the mail arrived it was full of past-due and collection notices.

Looking back on our situation, there were so many warning signs that we ignored because of our inexperience. In the same industry, but with much higher revenue, we have had fewer bad debts over the last eight years combined than we incurred in late 1987.

My partner and I had managed our personal finances reasonably well so we were able to secure second mortgages against our houses, but not without first having to send my wife for legal council because the house was in both of our names. Naturally the lawyer did his best to convince her not to allow me to remortgage the house. She didn't listen, so we invested more money in the business and bought out the third partner. We cut our pay so low that I had to sell my new car just so I could qualify for the increased mortgage payments.

In a period of two and a half years I put the same amount of money into that new car as I put into the down payment on my house. My mortgage payments were the same as rent or less because I had a tenant subsidizing the payments. When I sold the car I only had $200 after I paid out the lease, in the same two and a half years my home increased in value substantially. Since then I have spent very little on cars. I replaced my new car with one that was six years old, and although I was not very happy about it, these experiences really began the learning process for me.

It took some time and I lost a partner along the way, but within two years we had paid off our short-term debt, and one and a half years later we were completely debt free. The lessons we learned along the way made our company and ourselves more money than ever before and we still practise these methods today. It is hard to believe that only a few years ago I was totally broke with only one asset, my house. The company was $200,000 in debt and my personal debt had exceeded $200,000. Today the only debt my wife and I have is the occasional business loan.

It was a very difficult time in my life, but getting out of debt is certainly one of the greatest accomplishments of my life. I had to learn as much as possible about getting out of debt even though there were very few resources available to teach me. I had to get very creative and do things I did not even think I was capable of; but then again, I was already in a situation I thought I could never get myself into.

I have made some good decisions but I have made many more mistakes. I really have learned the hard way. It is difficult to put a dollar figure on what my ignorance has cost me in my working life, but I am certain my net worth would be two to three times what it is today, had I known then what I know now. I hope you learn from my mistakes so you do not experience the setbacks that I have experienced.

Can You Manage Your Debt?

With a bit of knowledge you can probably manage a great deal more debt than you realize. I make this point not to encourage you to increase your debt, but to enforce the idea that it can be quite easy to manage credit and debt once you know how. It is not entirely your fault if you find yourself with an uncomfortable amount of debt. Statistics show that Canadians are using credit more than ever before. In fact, Visa and MasterCard credit card debt alone has increased from an unpaid balance of $11.4 billion in October 1992 to $18.7 billion by October 1996. This is a massive 64 percent increase in unpaid debt in only four years. The long-term effects of this are very alarming.

When the Canada Pension Plan began, two things which were not anticipated at the time were the slowdown in birth rates after the baby boom ended, and the fact that people are living longer. As you are probably already aware, this has left us with some very serious shortages in funding. I don't expect the government will be able to look after us in the future, so you will likely be supporting your parents while trying to raise your own family and sending your children to college, not to mention trying to save for your retirement.

Do you know how to handle credit?

Unfortunately becoming burdened with debt is how most people eventually learn how to deal with debt. It is usually a trial and error process. None of us have been educated in our schools or universities on how to handle credit, or what is an appropriate use of credit. You could ask your banker, but unless they really know you, how do you know if the advice you are getting is in your best interest. Businesses go to great lengths to separate you from your money. You are the focus of hundreds of credit granters fighting each other for your business. You can not read a newspaper, a magazine, watch television, or listen to your radio without seeing or hearing several advertisements for banks, credit card companies, finance companies, or furniture stores offering credit cards or lines of credit. It never ends. Everyone is telling you, "You can have it all right now." Well you can, but you may be paying for it for years and it may be broken or worn out before it is paid off. Or if you stop paying, your creditors will come and take it away from you. Retailers and financial institutions do not care about your financial well-being, provided they are collecting their money, the retailers just want to sell their products, and the finance companies just want to collect their interest, nothing else matters. You can not even buy a container of milk in a grocery store without having to walk all the way to the back of the store passing numerous items along the way. This is no coincidence: it is designed to get you to buy as much as possible.

You would think the government would want us to be properly educated in financial matters; then again, look at the situation our government is in. Just imagine what it would be like if everyone was properly trained to deal with their finances. You would probably reduce bankruptcies by 90 percent, which would reduce costs to business, and the savings could be passed on to consumers. Do you realize there are people out there, and perhaps you're one of them, who could buy a house with the monthly payments they are paying on car loans, credit cards, furniture loans, etc.? Imagine how strong our economy would be if people did not get themselves into financial difficulties. In fact many economists tell us the reason the economy is still weak now is because consumers are so far in debt they can not afford to purchase new items. Until people start spending more money, the economy will never fully recover. Of course, they must have the money before they can spend it.

People who know how to use credit properly spend their money on goods and services, not interest payments, or they use credit to earn income. But if you're reading this you're probably not ready for that. The fastest way to get what you really want is to get out of debt first.

■ ■ ■ ■ ■ ■ **FOR INSTANCE** ■ ■ ■ ■ ■ ■

To understand fully what debt is costing you, consider the following example. If you are paying $100 per month in fees and interest payments, this is the equivalent of what you would pay on a small car loan of approximately $12,000, or on a department store credit balance of approximately $4000-4500. To get that $100 per month after taxes, most Canadians must earn $143 pretax per month or $1716 per year. That $100 per month equals $1200 per year, or a good vacation, or money you could invest in an RRSP. Your $100 per month for one year invested in an RRSP would reduce your taxes at your marginal rate (highest rate of tax you pay on your last dollar earned) by approximately $516, which will compound tax free as long as you keep it in your RRSP. If you continue to invest $100 a month for five years at eight percent you would have accumulated $7370.83 in your RRSP and reduced your taxes by approximately $2580 for a total of $9950.83.

■ ■

This simple example illustrates how debt limits your lifestyle today and in the future.

Danger Signs to
Watch Out For

$ You use credit cards for purchases that you used to pay for with cash.

$ You have reached or exceeded your credit card limits.

$ You can only afford the minimum payment on your credit cards.

$ You are unable to make payments on all your bills every month.

$ You have already consolidated your debt, but instead of reducing your debt you are still increasing it.

$ You would be in immediate financial crisis if you suddenly became unemployed.

$ You have started borrowing from family or friends to meet your financial needs.

$ You have no money in reserve for unexpected emergencies.

If you are experiencing any of the above, you could be setting yourself up for the ultimate financial crisis: personal bankruptcy.

Determining your net worth

On pages 12 and 13 there is a personal balance worksheet. The purpose of this worksheet is to determine your net worth. Your net worth is the sum of the value of your assets (what you own), less the liability (the debt you have accumulated to acquire them). You must be reasonable and not overvalue your assets, because if you do, you will only be fooling yourself. It's important to know your net worth because this is the measure which best evaluates your financial well being. In our society we tend to measure a person's financial status by the type of car they drive, the size of their home or the neighbourhood in which they live, but this is not the whole story; the personal balance worksheet will tell the whole story. Your personal balance worksheet will give you a starting point from which you can keep track of your progress as your situation improves. Without it you will never really know if your situation is improving.

Some things to consider while you fill out your personal balance worksheet: list all your assets at current market value, include everything like family emblems of value, art work, coin or stamp collections, etc. Also list all outstanding balances on all your debts including credit card balances, student loans, mortgages, and loans from family members. Finally, if you have a leased vehicle, enter its current market value as an asset and enter the buy out as a liability.

This will take some time to do properly and it should be updated on a monthly basis, so I have included a column for your loan number. I found from experience if I could give my banker or lease company my loan number they could enter it into their computer and tell me the current principal (outstanding balance), and what portion of my most recent payment went to interest and principal.

Two good reasons for filling out your personal balance worksheet

Filling out the personal balance worksheet can have a profound effect on you. If you were thinking of skipping over it go back and do it because it is one of the most important steps in the book, for two reasons. First, when you finish, line 25 represents your total net worth; but it represents much more than just that. This figure on line 25 represents everything you have accomplished in your life from a financial point of view. This is you right now! Now take the number of years you have worked and divide it into your net worth and you get an average of what you have accomplished on an annual basis from a financial point of view. I'll bet you're asking yourself, "Where did all the money go?" Or, "Is this all I have to show for _____ years of work?"

The second reason this worksheet is so important is because one day you will want to, or have to, retire and the lifestyle you live during your retirement will be directly related to your personal net worth. All over the world governments are realizing that with a large aging baby boom population, combined with longer life expectancies, they will not be able to fulfil their promises regarding retirement benefits for seniors. I don't think they will disappear completely, but I do believe that you will have to be living at or under the poverty line to qualify for them.

■ ■

PERSONAL BALANCE SHEET

Assets

1. Real estate value $_____

2. Chequing accounts $_____

3. Savings accounts $_____

4. Stocks/Bonds $_____

5. Insurance cash value $_____

6. Pension plan $_____

7. RRSPs $_____

8. Vehicles $_____

9. Home furnishings $_____

10. Collectibles $_____

11. Other $_____

12. The total of lines 1 to 11 equals your total assets $_____

Liabilities

	Creditor	Loan Number	Monthly Payment	Balance
13.	_____	_____	$_____	$_____
14.	_____	_____	$_____	$_____
15.	_____	_____	$_____	$_____
16.	_____	_____	$_____	$_____
17.	_____	_____	$_____	$_____
18.	_____	_____	$_____	$_____
19.	_____	_____	$_____	$_____
20.	_____	_____	$_____	$_____
21.	_____	_____	$_____	$_____
22.	_____	_____	$_____	$_____

23. Total monthly payments $_____

24. The total of lines 13 to 22 equals your total
 liabilities. $_____

 Subtract your total liabilities, line 24,
 from your total assets, line 12.

25. THIS EQUALS YOUR NET WORTH $_____

■ ■

Credit and Debt Management

The very first thing you must do is spend less money than you are taking home each month. As long as you are spending more than what you are earning, your situation will continue to get worse. If you have been spending more than you are earning you are living beyond your means. You may have already found that you can do this for a short period of time, but ultimately it will lead to a financial crisis.

Start recording all your daily expenses immediately. Get a small notepad to record **everything**, or use the worksheet provided on pages 20 and 21. Don't just record that you took $40 cash from the bank machine, record **everything you spent it on**. When you do this you will instantly change the way you spend your money. You reach a new level of accountability to yourself. I don't record my expenses all the time, but I should. Once when I had not been recording them and then started again I had developed a new habit of drinking caffe lattes, which I absolutely love, but I was drinking three large ones a day at a cost of almost nine dollars per day. When I started to write this down on my notebook, after three days I stopped buying them.

Categorize your expenses monthly and you will probably be surprised by how much money you wasted. You will be able to identify areas where you can reduce your spending. Don't wait until the end of the month, start right now and go through last month's chequebook and credit card statements, and try to recall as many of your cash expenses as possible.

Keep in mind that most businesses do this every day and produce a financial statement every month. Without this information the owners would never know whether they were profitable or not, and it helps them make adjustments to maintain profitability. You have to do the same, any profit (leftover money) is additional money that you can use to pay off your debt. Keeping track of expenses will identify areas of wastage. I had an employee who was always broke and had bill collectors calling him all the time. He had only a small amount of debt and could have paid it off easily, he spent more on cigarettes in a year than he owed but he never put the priority on paying off his debt. Money management is really about managing your priorities.

The monthly expense record on pages 20 and 21 has a numbered column from 1 to 31 representing each day in the month. There are also seven columns from left to right for you to record different categories of expenses. Use the top line to identify the category and every day record all your expenses. What you really want to be recording on the top line are your non-fixed expenses, so instead of using a column for rent or mortgage or car payment use them for things like lunches, coffee breaks, entertainment, alcohol, cigarettes, shopping sprees, and any other impulse spending like my caffe lattes. At the end of the month you can total them up and review your spending habits, and compare them month to month.

It's not how much you make, it's how much you save.

This statement could not be any simpler or more true. However, you can't usually save if you are in debt because your savings won't earn as much as you are paying in interest. For a debtor, your savings are all the extra money you can put on your debt. If you are in a 45 percent tax bracket and have an unpaid balance on a credit card charging 18 percent, by paying off the balance (thus eliminating the interest charges) you are effectively getting the same as a 33 percent return on your investment. If you have a department store card charging 28 percent and compounding monthly, it is the same as a 32 percent interest rate because you are paying interest on interest, not just principal. Paying this card off would be the same as getting a 56 percent return on your investment.

There is one exception, depending upon your present debt and your present rate of income tax: because savings within an RRSP are tax sheltered, by putting your savings into a RRSP you could reduce your taxes and then pay your debt with your tax refund.

■ ■ ■ ■ ■ ■ **FOR INSTANCE** ■ ■ ■ ■ ■ ■

You have $10,000 saved and a loan of $5000. You want to pay off the loan and put the balance in an RRSP. If you are in a 45 percent tax bracket you would end up with a $5000 RRSP, $5000 debt paid and a refund for $2250 from Revenue Canada. This is a substantial savings: $2250 in tax, turning your $10,000 into $12,250, plus all the interest you would have paid on your loan. However, if you have not been paying your maximum allowable contribution into your RRSP the carry-over rules would apply. This allows you to exceed your current years allowable contribution and add previous years contributions to the current year. If you have room for the entire $10,000 in there, and then use the tax refund to pay off the debt you would have a $10,000 RRSP and $4500 tax return to pay off your debt. You would still owe $500 on your debt, but you would have turned your $10,000 into $14,500 instead of the previous example of $12,250. If you are not certain of making a decision like this on your own, get advice from your accountant. If you do not have one, implementing this strategy alone would pay an accountant's fees for years, or consider writing out all the questions you have for an accountant and pay for an hour of their time to get the answers you need.

■ ■

Right now your savings should be used to pay off your debt in the most effective way. You should set your goal for having 20 percent of your income left over at the end of the month, which you can use to accelerate the payment on your debt. If you can afford more, apply as much as you can. When we were in debt, my wife and I spent 65 percent of our take-home income to reduce our debt. We were obviously making some sacrifices, but we are still in a lovely home which exceeds our needs, have two cars and are debt free in our mid-thirties.

After you have recorded your expenses, you are ready for a budget. Budgets are more effective after you have completed the expense recording exercise because you get a clearer picture of your spending habits and can produce a more realistic budget. The more realistic your budget, the easier it will be to stick to it. To set up a budget that will reduce your monthly expenses with the least amount of pain or sacrifice, use the worksheet on pages 22 and 23.

How much does it really cost?

You must realize the cost of credit. You can not determine whether or not something is affordable by only considering the minimum monthly payment or lease payments. Institutions charge very high interest rates and can be irresponsible when it comes to granting credit. You likely know someone who earns an average income, drives a leased car, and uses half a dozen or more credit cards with limits equal to half or more of their annual salary. It will take them forever to pay off the cards unless they drastically change their spending habits. This is exactly what finance companies want; the longer it takes you to pay something off the better it is for them.

If you use credit to get a bargain when you are short of cash, but you can't pay the bill when it is due, your bargain purchase will eventually cost more than the regular price. It doesn't take as long as you may think, just over a year of financing on a department store credit card will eat up a 25 percent discount. This applies to every purchase you make when you don t reduce your credit card balance. You could be a very thrifty shopper saving 25 percent on every purchase. However, if you just keep increasing your balance, over a four-year period you would actually pay more than twice the regular price of your 25-percent-off purchase, or three times the sale price. What a bargain!

MONTHLY EXPENSE RECORD

	Caffe Lattes	Lunches	Groceries	Vehicle	Entertainment	Clothing	Other
1							
2							
3							
4							
5							
6							
7							
8							
9							
10							
11							
12							
13							
14							
15							

16
17
18
19
20
21
22
23
24
25
26
27
28
29
30
31
Ttl.

■ ■

MONTHLY BUDGET

Net Income	Annual	Monthly
Your income	$_____	$_____
Your spouse's income	$_____	$_____
Family allowance	$_____	$_____
Other income	$_____	$_____
Total net income	$_____	$_____
A. Total average monthly income		$_____

Regular Monthly Expenses	Estimated	Actual
Rent or mortgage, including property taxes	$_____	$_____
Utilities, phone, power, heat, cable, etc.	$_____	$_____
Food and household goods	$_____	$_____
Loan payments	$_____	$_____
Transportation expenses, bus, car, taxis, etc.	$_____	$_____
Child-care expenses, day-care, baby-sitters	$_____	$_____
Clothing	$_____	$_____
Health needs, prescription drugs	$_____	$_____
Insurance, life, disability, etc.	$_____	$_____
Alimony, child support	$_____	$_____
Work expenses	$_____	$_____
Personal, cosmetics, haircuts, etc.	$_____	$_____
Recreation, sports, fitness clubs, etc.	$_____	$_____

Regular Monthly Expenses	Estimated	Actual
Entertainment, liquor, movies, restaurants, etc.	$_____	$_____
Subscriptions, newspapers, etc.	$_____	$_____
Vacation fund	$_____	$_____
Retirement fund	$_____	$_____
Other	$_____	$_____
B. Total	$_____	$_____

A – B (income less expenses)
= money available to apply to debt $_____

■ ■

Some credit card companies justify interest rates of 20 to 30 percent (which are actually even higher, depending on how often they are "compounded"), by telling credit-worthy customers that they need these high rates to cover bad debts (from people who do not pay their bills), and fraud. Well, they are the ones granting the credit. If they did not give just anyone a credit card they would not have this problem.

The fact that credit card debt is unsecured debt certainly justifies increased interest rates. In the case of a car loan or mortgage, which is secured by the car or house, the finance company can at least repossess the security, but it is pretty hard to repossess last month's night on the town. In my opinion, however, some interest rates are too high, especially if you consider how banks set those rates. They are based on the prime rate, which is set by the Bank of Canada, then the banks usually add one to three percent. Visa and MasterCard traditionally would add about nine or ten percent until about 1994, now they are adding approximately 13 percent. They have not raised their interest rate, they just haven't followed the prime rate down, which is widening the gap. Department store cards add up to 20 percent or more.

As long as these institutions are advertising in places like university campuses and aiming at students who are already struggling to get by, they will never get my sympathy. They are doing the equivalent of handing out a shovel and helping students dig their own financial graves before they even begin their working careers. You do not see them doing much about controlling fraud either. Something as simple as your photograph on your credit card, like City Bank Visa recently started in the United States, or using a pin number, such as the one on your bank card, with a credit card could help reduce such fraud. It sure makes me wonder if it is just an excuse to justify ridiculous interest rates.

It's your nickel and your neck

In personal as well as business partnerships it is common to jointly borrow money, but if the lender is legally demanding repayment, they may only be able to seize personal property from one of the borrowers to cover the debt. This leaves this person in a position where they would have to sue their partner in order to recover their partner's portion of the debt. So remember, you alone are responsible for your finances, so you can't allow anyone else to influence or make decisions for you regarding the amount of debt you are comfortable with. When the creditors come looking for their money they do not care whose idea it was, or who talked you into borrowing it, they will be looking for you. Make certain you are the one making the financial decisions regarding your credit and not someone else. If you feel that someone else is committing you to borrow more money than you are comfortable with, trust those feelings, you are right. It is your life, your credit, your reputation, and your sleepless nights.

There is a way you can deal with a situation like this if you are in a business partnership. When structuring your financing you can limit the amount of financing each partner is personally guaranteeing based on their portion of shares they own in the company. Then back this up with a shareholders' agreement using a similar formula, as well as having a default clause which will give the shareholders a clear direction to take. This is not as complicated as it sounds, but a shareholders' agreement is an absolute must have if you are in a business partnership. If you don't have one get your lawyer and your partners together and get an agreement signed.

Do's and don'ts

Only use credit when it is absolutely necessary: for a car to get you to work, a home, or an emergency. Never use credit for...

- $ clothes
- $ food
- $ vacations
- $ furniture
- $ electronic goods
- $ bills

You should pay cash for all these items. If you have been using credit to purchase these items you are probably using your credit to get you through to the end of the month. The problem is, your situation will be even worse next month. You must stop this immediately. This is a serious financial trap. You can't get yourself into a situation where you are spending so much of your money paying all your bills that not enough is left to survive until the next payday, forcing you to go further into debt. Nobody wants to live from paycheque to paycheque, we never know what could happen in the future. A good example of a financial trap is falling for one of these "buy now and don't pay for six months" offers when you buy a new stereo and CD player. You figure you have six months to save the money to pay the bill when it comes due, but if you are like most people you will spend all your money on new CDs and take a couple years to pay off your stereo. Be smart, don't set yourself up. If you can save enough in six months, save the money first and pay cash.

Help yourself to plan for these large expenditures with an annual budget plan, using the worksheet on page 30. You can actually pay less cash because the retailers offering these no-interest deals will give you a discount equal to the interest cost on the item you are purchasing and all you have to do is ask for it.

Understanding the calculations

Just because your loans officer qualifies you for a loan, that doesn't mean you have to borrow all of it. The calculations used to determine whether you qualify for a loan are based on your gross debt service ratio. They determine how much more debt you can handle based on what percentage of your income is needed to cover your living expenses, such as housing and vehicle costs, and your current debt, usually 32 to 40 percent depending on your previous credit history and income level.

■ ■ ■ ■ ■ ■ **FOR INSTANCE** ■ ■ ■ ■ ■ ■

If your monthly income was $3000 your debt service ratio would be between $960 and $1200 per month. A monthly servicing cost of your credit card debt is established by including a monthly payment of usually only five percent of the outstanding balance, but this five percent amounts to next to no payment at all on the principal. You should pay 100 percent of your outstanding balance on your credit cards monthly. With these percentages you should be able to determine if you are trying to support too much debt or if you are only carrying a comfortable amount of debt, simply by determining your debt service ratio and subtract your current monthly payments. If the debt load is too high you should liquidate some of the items which are costing too much, and if you can afford more you should consider increasing your payments to accelerate the repayment of your debt.

■ ■

You should never increase your debt if you can't pay off your current short-term debt, especially and including all the debt on your credit cards. If you borrow money when you can't pay off your credit card balance each month you are setting yourself up for a financial disaster. If you can't pay off your balance monthly, and you borrow more money (which will use up more of your monthly income) to service the new debt, what are you going to pay off your credit card with?

Every day loans officers lend money to people who can't pay off their credit card debt, or don't want to pay it off, or haven't even considered paying it off. Remember, lenders profit from our interest payments, so they like us to take our time when paying off debt.

Canada Mortgage and Housing Corporation (CMHC) has recently reduced the amount they will loan to individuals based on their debt service ratio due to concerns of increased credit card debt. We can hope that the banks will follow their lead and take credit card debt more seriously when people are applying for loans.

Consider the cost of lost opportunity

If you borrow the maximum amount of money available to you based on your gross debt service ratio what will it cost in terms of not being able to act on opportunities? If you decide to use it all for a car and commit yourself to a five-year loan, chances are you won't be able to purchase anything else on credit for the next five-year period. When the five years is up, you will want a new car because your present one is old and out of date. You wouldn't want to sacrifice your standard of living by driving a five-year-old car! This cycle can go on forever. Opportunities come to people all the time. Very often people will say someone was lucky when they become successful, but these people were prepared to react when opportunities arose. Are you going to miss out on buying a car, a home, or a business at bargain prices because you are at your financial limit? Do you want to start your own business but can't because of debt? Are you willing to wait five or ten years to fulfil your dreams? If you can't make the sacrifices now, will you be able to in the future? There is a saying that goes something like this, "Success happens when preparation meets opportunity." Are you financially prepared?

Be prepared

Always be prepared for financial setbacks. If you have not had one yet, you certainly will have one and probably several in your lifetime. It is a fact of life that you could lose your job, have unexpected bills, experience a death, or a new addition, or a divorce in your family. There is always something, so be prepared for it. Do not use up all your resources; keep something available to you at all times so you can deal with these situations when they happen. You should always have at least one month's income in savings available to you for emergencies. Some people suggest up to three month's income, but I believe one month is adequate and that the extra two month's income would be more useful paying down your Visa or MasterCard or your

MAJOR HOUSEHOLD EXPENDITURES

This worksheet is for anticipated household expenditures. The objective is to start a savings plan which will cover the cost of the expenditure by the time you need the items.

Item	Planned Purchase Date	Amount Saved	Total Required
1. _____	_____	$ _____	$ _____
		$ _____	
		$ _____	
		$ _____	
2. _____	_____	$ _____	$ _____
		$ _____	
		$ _____	
		$ _____	
3. _____	_____	$ _____	$ _____
		$ _____	
		$ _____	
		$ _____	

4. _____ $ _____ _____ _____ $ _____
   $ _____
   $ _____
   $ _____

5. _____ $ _____ _____ _____ $ _____
   $ _____
   $ _____
   $ _____

6. _____ $ _____ _____ _____ $ _____
   $ _____
   $ _____
   $ _____

7. _____ $ _____ _____ _____ $ _____
   $ _____
   $ _____
   $ _____

personal creditline. Then it is still accessible in an emergency by way of a cash advance, but if you don't have an emergency you will be reducing your overall interest costs, which will get you out of debt faster. As you reduce your debt, and increase your savings, your finances will be increasingly more stable.

Since I started writing this book, a series of things happened that I did not anticipate: I received a bill from Revenue Canada, a recent holiday cost more than expected, we did some damage to the car that we wanted to fix ourselves to avoid an insurance premium increase, Christmas was coming, and my wife was expecting. Take it from me, there will always be setbacks, so have something set aside to cover them. A series of events like this would have been devastating for us a few years ago, now when something unforeseen happens my wife and I reluctantly go to the bank and take the money out of our joint savings account to pay for it all.

Fail to plan, Plan to fail

Fail to plan, plan to fail. This is a rule that I live by. Look at the big picture: are you going to be in the same situation in one, two, or five years from now? Or are you going to be in an even worse financial situation? Will you be in a better situation? With interest charges adding up daily, the longer you put off paying your debt, the worse your situation will get and the more difficult it will become.

"Most people spend more time planning their vacation than their financial future." Not my quote but one I have heard often. Whatever amount of debt you have, you must make a plan to pay it off now. You are the one who must make this decision. The decisions you make now will determine what your financial situation will be in one, two, or five years from now. You must have a plan to reduce and eliminate all of your debt.

In the late '70s and early '80s inflation was high and people were getting annual raises of ten percent or higher. Chances are only one of your parents worked and they had one or two careers throughout their lifetime. This gave people some comfort when they arranged a loan, but these days are gone, probably forever. Today, we have downsizing, rightsizing, corporate takeovers and mergers, inflation is very low and jobs are hard to get and harder to keep. People are getting very low raises and some are taking pay cuts just to keep their jobs. Less fortunate people are losing their jobs. Career changes can have a negative impact on your finances. The time to reduce your debt is now because your situation could get worse before it gets better. Be prepared, have a plan, and also have a backup plan. The following chapters will help you make a plan to reduce your debt.

Let's Get Started

In the previous chapters you should have filled out the budget and expense report. You will need to do it in order to get the most out of this chapter. You should have a much better understanding and some new ideas regarding the importance of properly managing your money, but now you need facts. If your budget is correct, and you don't have any money left over at the end of the month or your income is less than your expenses, or you are just looking for the best way to improve your current situation, then you must do some or all of the following...

- ⑤ consolidate debt to reduce your monthly expenses
- ⑤ sell off assets to repay some of your current debt
- ⑤ cut all luxuries out of your current monthly expenses
- ⑤ reduce your expenses
- ⑤ increase your income

Consolidation can really help

Consolidation is the most effective way to pay off debt, but it also requires the most discipline. By consolidating all or as many high-interest debts as possible, you can get one low-interest loan to pay off all the higher-interest debt. Consolidating can simplify your cash flow because you only have to make one payment each month instead of several payments at different times during the month. By reducing your overall monthly payments, you will get back to having your income greater than your outflow. Consolidation is ideal for people who have equity in other assets (such as cars or a home) to support the new loan.

Attaining a consolidation loan of 18 to 24 months is great motivation because it gives you a time frame, a target whereby you see your progress every month. If you use this approach, for example to pay off two or three credit cards, you could cut the amount of interest in half or even better. This would enable you to get out of debt that much faster. Sometimes you can get an interest-free loan from a parent or family member, but if you do not repay this loan be aware that it can cause a tremendous amount of stress in your family. Your best place to attain a consolidation loan is from one of the major banks in the form of a personal credit line or fixed loan.

Be sure that you don't run up bills again. If you have a problem with credit card spending, cut up your credit cards. This is why discipline is so important: if you don't control your spending, consolidating your debt will not reduce your debt. Without discipline you could have your credit cards to the maximum again and still be paying for the consolidation loan you originally acquired to pay them off. Beware that you do not roll all your debt into a low-interest loan or mortgage;

if the loan or mortgage is for a long period of time, you could end up paying even more interest. For example, if your mortgage is due and you decide to pay off your credit cards by adding the debt to your mortgage, you may cut your interest rate in half. But if it takes you 15 or 20 years to pay off your mortgage, you will be paying substantially more interest than you would have had you just paid your credit cards off over one or two years.

Sell off your assets

Make a list of your assets and see if you can rearrange some of them. Perhaps you have some items which are no longer useful to you, but could be of value to someone else. Like the saying goes, "One man's junk is another man's treasure." If so, sell those unnecessary items and use the money to pay down your debts. Maybe that car of yours is two or three times as expensive as your needs require, or maybe you do not need a car at all.

Perhaps you have a Canada Savings Bond, or some other investment, or a savings account earning a small amount of interest. This interest is taxable as income at your highest rate, because it is taxed just like any other income. However, unlike your other income on which you pay taxes at source, (your employer withholds the income tax portion of your pay and submits it to Revenue Canada) there has been no tax paid on interest income, which has always been considered taxable income unless it was inside your RRSP. This income could put you into a higher tax bracket, reducing your tax refund even more. Interest income has always been considered taxable income unless it was inside your RRSP. Since the 1994 budget the federal government removed the $100,000 personal capital gains exemption so stocks and mutual funds are also taxable. You may consider these investments as a backup or emergency fund. But as I mentioned earlier, if you pay off the unpaid balance on your credit card or loan, which would increase your cash flow and save money on interest payments, you would still have the credit available to you for an emergency.

■ ■ ■ ■ ■ ■ **FOR INSTANCE** ■ ■ ■ ■ ■ ■

If you have a $1000 balance in a savings account or a savings bond earning 3 to 5 percent interest per year. That's $30 - $50 per year before taxes. After taxes it would be approximately $20 - $35 per year. If you also have a credit card outstanding balance of $1000 you could be paying 20 - 30 percent interest or $200 - $300 per year in interest. Simply by using the savings to pay down the debt you could save approximately $180 - $260 per year.

■ ■ ■ ■ ■ ■ ■ ■ ■ ■ ■ ■ ■ ■ ■ ■ ■ ■ ■ ■

Cut out all luxuries

Many people spend too much of their money on expensive club memberships, or have other expensive habits and hobbies. We all like to travel, drive expensive sports cars, eat in fine restaurants, go to sporting events, participate in expensive sports, and so on. Some people try to accomplish all of these things during one vacation. The reality is that these are all luxuries you likely can't afford right now. People will often make decisions based on egos instead of practicality. Take some time to think about some of the decisions you have made in the past, you may regret some of them now. The trick is to identify clearly your motives when you make these decisions.

Reduce your expenses

You can save on virtually everything you spend money on without sacrificing quality. You probably already know several ways of reducing your expenses, but you may not be applying them. I was very surprised to find out how many insignificant things I could save money on. It may seem like a waste of time when you only consider each small cut in spending individually, but because there are so many, the savings combined will be substantial. Simply by taking a lunch to work instead of buying it could save you $4 or $5 a day or $80 a month. If there are two of you, that's $160 to $200 per month. If you drive to work every day, consider riding a bicycle or car pool with co-workers or friends who travel to and from the same area.

There are other ways you can reduce expenses. For example, before you go grocery shopping you should always do an inventory of your refrigerator and kitchen so you can purchase food that you can prepare with food you have already purchased. Then make a grocery list and stick to it. Try the lesser expensive brand names or no-name items as well, if you have never tried them you'll be surprised that some are better than brand names for much less money. And never go grocery shopping when you are hungry, when I do this I end up with a cart full of snack food that I can't make a proper meal with. We shop at a warehouse shopping club once a month and we treat it just like shopping for groceries with a list and we save a lot of money for a bit of inconvenience.

Try to follow buying cycles. Almost everything I can think of goes on sale and/or has a high and low price cycle. Sports cars and motorcycles are cheaper in fall and winter than spring and summer. Four-wheeled drive vehicles are cheaper in the spring and summer than fall and winter. Most retail items are cheaper on Boxing Day especially electronic goods and computers. Some of the best buys in furniture are from Boxing Day to the end of May. Clothing is always cheaper at the end of the season instead of the beginning. Retail stores always have to move out the current season's inventory to make room for the next season's inventory. They start discounting patio furniture in late June and early July to make room for fall and winter stock.

I'm not suggesting you don't celebrate Christmas because items cost less on Boxing Day but if you need large ticket items you could spend less before Christmas and perhaps save 50 percent on a major purchase after Christmas.

Lately, there has been a lot of publicity on life insurance; whether to buy a term plan or a whole (universal) life policy. I personally think term policies are better for most people, especially if you are young and have a lot of debt. Just recently a friend of mine cancelled a whole life policy he had for four years. He paid $90 per month for a $250,000 policy. Upon termination he did not get any money back. If he had had a term policy, the cost would have been approximately $25 to $30 per month. When you cancel a term life insurance policy you don't get anything back either, but the $60 per month difference would be more effective paying off debt or invested in an RRSP where it can earn guaranteed tax free interest. Buy insurance as protection, not as an investment. If you have a whole or universal life policy you should consider what kind of a return you are getting, if it is taxable or not, and if you are capable of getting a better return by managing your own money.

These are just a few ideas you should think about that could save you a lot of money over time. I suggest you pick up a book or newsletter on penny-pinching or dollar-pinching. You will get more ideas than you'll know what to do with.

Increase your income

You may want to consider a part-time job. One of the very best I have heard of is to work as a delivery driver for a successful Chinese restaurant. This may seem unusual, but consider the facts. If you have bought your car with a car loan that is not tax deductible, by using the car for work you will be able to write off some of the interest on the loan, gas, insurance, and repairs. Another benefit of working for a successful Chinese restaurant is that the orders cost more than your typical pizza orders, so your tips are higher, and these restaurants usually close much earlier, allowing you to get a good night's sleep.

In some cases you can do extra work for your employer and use the additional money to pay off debt. If you get the opportunity to work overtime, you have to be disciplined. You could have a night on the town, or you could see that money multiply two or three times because of what it will save you in interest payments.

Perhaps you have a talent or skill that you could use to make more money. You could use this skill to start a small business and run it out of your home, which would qualify for several tax deductions. Consider renting out a room in your home, which would provide both income and a tax deduction. If you rent, bring in another room-mate to share the expenses. If you spend ten hours of your time reading a current tax planning guide and figured out how to save $500 in taxes, that equals $50 per hour after taxes for your time.

Prioritizing Your Debt

Now that you have made the changes necessary to increase your cash flow, the next step to getting out of debt is to reduce the amount of interest you are paying. This will obviously get you out of debt faster. The objective is to identify which debts are costing the most to service. On the worksheet on pages 46 and 47 you should record your present debt, the interest you are being charged, the amount of principal you are paying with each payment, the length of amortization of the loan and total amount paid. You may have to contact the financial institutions to find out some of this information, and it will take some time, but it will be a learning experience for you. Nothing will open your eyes faster than finding out how much interest you are actually paying. You also have to find out if there are any prepayment penalties and inquire about how much interest you will save by shortening your loans. You must ask about penalties because some lenders charge a premium for paying off a loan early.

A good example is an automobile lease or a mortgage where some of the lenders will make you pay all or a portion of the interest you would have paid had you just continued to pay it over time. Obviously there would be less incentive to pay off this debt. You also have to take into consideration whether the interest is tax deductible. Tax deductible debt means all or a portion of the interest can be used to reduce your taxable income, thus saving you money on your taxes. This applies to business loans, rental property mortgages, and car loans if the car is used for work. There are other areas where you may have tax deductible debt. If you are uncertain ask an accountant.

Pay off the loan with the highest interest first

Once you have all this information, you are ready to get started. Choose the loan or credit card with the highest interest rate and no penalty for prepayment (which is not tax deductible). Pay it off by increasing the payments or making bulk payments, which will go directly towards the principal. Definitely continue to make your payments on all your other debts, but if you plan to pay more than minimum payments on any other debt, it's better to use the additional money to pay as much as possible on the debt charging the highest interest. You may be tempted to load up on several of your debts, however, your money is maximized by paying the highest rate of interest first. Once your first debt is paid off, use the money you were using to service the first loan and apply it all to the next highest interest rate of a non-deductible debt. Continue this process until all of your debt is paid off. The last debt you want to pay off is the tax-deductible debt.

The following page is a debt worksheet. It is designed for you to record your creditor, the interest rate on the debt, the payment amount, the amount of the payment which is allocated to interest, the amount of the payment which is allocated to principal, how long the loan is for in months, and the total amount of interest you will be paying over the term of the loan. After you have completed the first part of the worksheet use the second part to list your creditors according to the highest rate of interest to the lowest. This will give you an action plan for the most effective way of paying off your debt.

DEBT WORKSHEET

	Creditor	Rate	Payment	Interest	Principal	Term	Total Interest
1							
2							
3							
4							
5							
6							
7							
8							
9							
10							
11							
12							

Once you have completed the first part of the worksheet, repeat the list again below, but this time in order of the highest interest rate to the lowest interest rate. This is your action plan for debt reduction.

Priority of Debts

	Creditor	Rate	Payment	Interest	Principal	Term	Total Interest
1							
2							
3							
4							
5							
6							
7							
8							
9							
10							
11							
12							

Credit Use and Abuse

The most common areas where people use and abuse credit are: credit and finance cards, car loans and leases, mortgages, student loans, and personal lines of credit.

Credit and charge cards

These days almost everyone has or has had a credit card. It is usually our first experience with credit and often results in disaster. In a way, you are being set up. The difficulty of using a credit card is that it requires a great deal of discipline.

A bulletin issued in May 1994 by Industry Canada (based on information supplied by the Canadian Bankers' Association) states that as of December 1993 there were an estimated 55 million credit cards in circulation in Canada, or 2.7 cards for every Canadian over the age of 18. Of those cards, 25 million are Visa or MasterCard. It is estimated that 50 percent are not paid off each month.

There has been so much controversy in Canada over credit card interest rates that in May 1986 the House of Commons issued an Order of Reference to the finance committee to study interest rates charged by issuers of credit cards and charge cards. The difference between a credit and charge card is that charge cards require payment in full every month. The original American Express card is a good example of a charge card.

I will not go into every detail of the finance committee's document, but there are some areas worth mentioning. The background paper took almost four pages to explain the calculation of interest charges on unpaid balances. Some issuers charge interest on the average daily balance retroactive to the posting dates. Some charge interest from the statement date; others, after a partial payment is made, charge interest on the total previous outstanding balance to either the posting dates or the statement date. Then there are other credit card companies that charge interest on the previous balance less the partial payment, if that payment is greater than 50 percent of the previous balance.

■ ■ ■ ■ ■ ■ **FOR INSTANCE** ■ ■ ■ ■ ■ ■

You may have a credit card with an unpaid balance of $2000, and you make a large payment of $1800 only to find out the following month that you are being charged interest on the previous $2000 balance instead of the current $200 balance. In other words, no matter what rate of interest is published on your statement you could be paying substantially more than that. If, on the other hand, this example was applied to a car loan, you would only have to pay the interest on the $200.

■ ■ ■ ■ ■ ■ ■ ■ ■ ■ ■ ■ ■ ■ ■ ■ ■ ■ ■ ■

I do not know whether it was the result of public outcry or pressure from the Canadian government, but as of April

1994 Visa and MasterCard in Canada charge lower fees and interest rates than in the United Kingdom or United States.

An example of just how long it can take to pay off a credit card by making only minimum payments was illustrated by a US news program. They did a show on the financial well-being of the baby boom generation now that many have reached their late forties and many aspire to retire early. They hired a financial expert to analyse the financial situation of three different couples. One couple had paid off their house but had eight credit cards with a balance of approximately $10,000. They figured that it would take over 20 years to pay that off if they only paid the minimum balance each month. Of course, these figures apply to the United States and not necessarily to Canada.

■ ■ ■ ■ ■ ■ **FOR INSTANCE** ■ ■ ■ ■ ■ ■

If we consider the cost of a car loan, for example $5000 over 3 years at $161 per month, you pay that and still have a car. However, if you owe $5000 on several credit cards but only have to pay a total minimum payment of perhaps $150 per month, many card holders will only pay the $150. You must realise that, depending on the interest rate you are being charged, as little as $65 from your $150 payment is actually going to principal and the other $85 is only paying interest.

■ ■

As your balance reduces so does your minimum monthly payment requirements, which increases the amount of time it will take to pay off the debt. There is no fixed term on a credit card debt, which means that you will have to continue to pay for the credit card. Get out your credit card statements and look at the charges. Do you want to pay off your bills from last Christmas or last month's night out or last year's vacation over perhaps as many as 10 years or longer at interest rates of between 9.70 and 30 percent?

Another important consideration when using credit cards is impulse buying. Research has proven that people will spend more using a credit card than with cash. Retailers benefit from this every day. In order to cash in on impulse buying, the latest trend in retailing is for retailers to offer their own credit cards. Major department stores, electronics stores and furniture stores offer credit cards or finance cards. Some department stores will only take cash, cheques, or their own credit cards because they want to earn interest off your credit card debt in addition to the money they make selling their goods to you. Department stores and gasoline retailers generally charge much higher rates than Visa or MasterCard, 28 to 30 percent per year interest is not uncommon with retailers. Visa and MasterCard charge approximately 10 percent annual interest for their low rate cards and 17 percent annual interest for their regular cards.

Retailers are even getting impulse buyers in the privacy of their own homes. When was the last time you watched your favourite TV program and were assaulted by someone trying to sell you something? In fact advertising on television is so successful there are informercials whereby companies buy half an hour to an hour of television time in order to sell you something. The ultimate advertising medium in television are the home shopping channels. There is only one reason they run these commercials and that is because they are successful. Have you noticed that none of the programs accept C.O.D. payments anymore? The reason is simple, impulse buyers make up a very large share of their market. If these purchasers had the opportunity to back out of the deal, as they could in a C.O.D. situation, a large number of purchasers would do so.

Credit cards can be useful

Credit cards do have a time and place, of course. They are wonderful in a crisis situation because of your ability to have quick access to money and an optional time frame to pay it off. But if you are at your maximum credit amount, you can't even use the card for what should be its primary use. What I consider a crisis is having to book an airline ticket because of a death in the family, or if your car breaks down and without a vehicle you would lose your job, or if your furnace quits in the middle of January and you need to replace it immediately.

It isn't really necessary to have more than one card. All you need is a Visa or MasterCard, both are accepted almost everywhere, and you will establish a good credit rating by paying your statement every month. Your payment habits are recorded at the Credit Bureau and are accessible to virtually all credit granters.

Just recently, no fee, low interest Visa and MasterCard have been offered by several banks. These are your best bet if you are unable to pay them off quickly. However, this is only a band-aid, not a solution. I tell you about them reluctantly because I am completely against the use of credit when you cannot pay off your present debt. But I also realize the fact that you may be just beginning to tackle this matter and it will take you some time to get your finances in order. Some of the banks will let you transfer your balance directly from a regular rate Visa or MasterCard to a low rate card which would reduce the amount of interest. The money you save on interest could then be applied to the debt.

Also available now, and I personally would not use one, are the GM and Ford credit cards. GM offers five percent of the cost of your purchase off the cost of a new car up to a maximum of $3500. But to qualify for the $3500, you would have to spend $70,000 on your credit card over a seven-year period. The Ford card operates in much the same way. Anyone who is in financial difficulty does not need another reason to use a credit card. You and I both know some people, perhaps even ourselves, who are more motivated to use their credit cards when they are rewarded with points or air miles and this is exactly why they have these rewards programs. If you want to save money on vehicles, I will show you a strategy that will save you thousands of dollars and does not include buying new cars.

You don't have to pay interest

Remember, interest rates do not apply when you pay off your credit card every month. The bottom line on credit cards is you only need one, and you should pay it off every month on or before the due date. If you can't, you shouldn't have one. It may sound slightly drastic but you may want to consider keeping your credit card in a safety deposit box, or in a cup of water frozen in your freezer. This way you will still have the card available for emergencies. It will also minimize your impulse buying because by the time you can get to your card, you will probably have changed your mind about what you were about to purchase. Almost everyone has an item of clothing in their closet that they have never even worn (including myself) and which probably would never have been purchased if you did not have a credit card.

One way to control your credit card spending and ensure that you can pay off your bill every month is to record in your cheque book every time you use your credit card, just as if you were writing a cheque. You wouldn't write a cheque if you didn't have the money, so you apply that same attitude towards your credit cards. When your bill comes you would simply add up the entries in your cheque book and write the cheque to pay off all the new charges. Perhaps even better, if you don't like to carry cash, and like the convenience of a credit card, use a debit card.

Positive aspects of credit cards

Other than having funds available in an emergency, your credit card can actually make you money. First you have to be in a position where you are debt free.

■ ■ ■ ■ ■ ■ **FOR INSTANCE** ■ ■ ■ ■ ■ ■

Let's say you wanted to buy a new television set. You save the money for the new set but instead of paying cash, you put the cost of the TV on your Visa or Master-Card and put the cash in an interest-earning account until the bill is due. If you know the statement cut-off date, you could purchase merchandise the day after and collect interest for approximately seven to eight weeks. For example, if my cut-off date is the 21st of every month, I could make a purchase on June 22 for $700. Since the bill won't arrive until approximately August 4 and won't be due until August 12, I could put the $700 in a term or savings account on June 22, and collect interest until August 11, at which time I pay the bill in full. I did not pay any interest because I paid the card in full, but I have earned interest on my money while using the credit card company's money.

■ ■

Three years ago I started using a credit card which gives air miles on a designated airline. I benefit from this in two ways. First, because I own my own business I can pay some of my creditors with my credit card and extend my payable another 40-45 days, and still keep them happy. Second, this more than doubles the amount I put on the card and I earn air miles that much faster. This sounds good, but it is not the card for everyone. Remember, I pay the card off every month and I also pay $95 annually for the card. I also put a large number of expenses on it. If you cannot accumulate more than 20,000 air miles annually, you may be spending as much or more on the annual premium as you would save in airline tickets.

When used properly a credit card can be your best friend. As you can see from our previous examples, they can make or save you money, they are almost always necessary if you want to rent a car or hotel room or get a membership at your local video store, and they are excellent for travelling, allowing you to carry only minimum amounts of cash. If you are travelling through several countries, you never need worry about constantly exchanging your cash from one currency to another. Visa automatically calculates it for you and the exchange rates are usually better. If you use cash or traveller's cheques you sometimes end up changing dollars to pounds to marks to lira, and when you get home, back to dollars. This gets very expensive because you pay a fee every time you make the exchange.

Credit cards are also excellent for record keeping since you receive a detailed statement at the end of each month. If you are required to record your monthly expenses for your employer or your small business, even if you lose the original receipt you will receive your backup statement to prove the expense existed.

Is leasing a car a good choice?

A car is usually the second largest purchase most people make, the first being a house. It is also a process which most people will go through several times in their life and yet may be paying far more than they have to. Leasing to buy can be a serious mistake. You have seen plenty of ads for $10,000 cars for only $200 per month, but this is for a 60-month lease. When the lease is up and you still don't own the car, you need to pay the "buy out," which is the balance or amount still outstanding on the vehicle. To continue to pay no more than $200 per month you will probably need a 24-month loan. You end up paying $200 per month for 84-months or $16,800 for a $10,000 car that will be seven years old when it is finally paid off. Very likely, after three years the warranty will expire as well. You probably couldn't find anyone who would find this acceptable, but that is essentially what you are doing when you are leasing.

In other words, a lease is virtually renting a car for a long period of time, or essentially having someone else get the financing for you and then marking up the cost of both the car and the financing. With any lease of 48 months or longer, you could find yourself worse off than you started if your needs change and you have to get out of the lease. Even if you have already been making payments for two years, you may be surprised to find out that you probably can't even sell the car for enough money to buy out the lease. Because the vehicle was purchased new and carries an additional surcharge for leasing, it will depreciate faster than you can pay it off.

Some salespeople will tell you leasing doesn't tie up your money or that it will not affect your borrowing power. But as you already know, bankers grant loans based on a gross debt service ratio and, yes, they do consider your lease payments the same as a loan payment.

Two-seater sports cars are very popular with men and women these days, however, they have the highest turn-over rate mainly because people's needs change. These cars are fun, but if you suddenly become a new mother or father, or need your car for business reasons, they are virtually useless.

You could potentially get yourself into a situation where you purchase a new car and six months later it is damaged beyond repair. If properly insured, the insurance company will pay market value for the vehicle, but you can be sure that market value on a six-month-old vehicle is probably 15 to 20 percent less than what you just paid for the vehicle. Depending on your down payment, you may find yourself with a car loan and no car. Recently, insurance companies began offering replacement value policies for around $30 per year for the first two years of your new vehicle so you can protect yourself if this happens to you.

When I started my business I sold my car to raise cash and then leased a vehicle. Two years later I needed more money so I sold the leased vehicle. After two and a half years of payments I only had $200 after I paid out the lease. I had spent more than $10,000 on payments on that car, so you see, I learned the hard way.

I still needed a vehicle so I purchased a six-year-old car and had it checked out by a mechanic. I drove it for about two years and put about 40,000 miles on it, then sold it for $1000 more than I paid for it. In the two years that I had it, I spent approximately $1035 in repairs, so the entire cost of owning this car was about $35. Not bad considering the previous one cost about $10,000 to drive the same length of time. If you can find a car approximately six to ten years old, in good condition, and you keep it in good condition, it will lose little or no value and may even increase in value.

Automobile manufacturers and dealers are the only people who consistently make money on vehicles. You will probably lose money on every vehicle you own. Under normal circumstances, vehicles cost money in two ways: first by depreciation and secondly by their repairs. So you get to choose which way to lose money: a new $30,000 vehicle will depreciate faster than a five-year-old $8,000 vehicle, but the latter will likely cost more in repairs. The difference is that your total annual costs for payment, repairs, and overall depreciation will be much lower on the older vehicle.

Check out a used car carefully

If you are buying a used vehicle from a private seller, whether it is two years old or several years old, try to buy one that has never been involved in an accident, still has its original paint, has a service history, and is still under warranty. Have the vehicle checked out by a qualified mechanic, contact the dealer to see if the warranty is up to date, and do a lien check. If there is a lien, your payment must be to the registered owner and the lien holder. Make sure that your payment is greater than the lien balance or you could be taking over the seller's debt.

Ask the seller why they are selling the vehicle. If they are upgrading to a newer vehicle they have probably, but not necessarily, serviced the vehicle on a regular basis. If they are selling because they can't afford to keep it, then there is a chance that it hasn't been serviced properly. I always avoid repossessed vehicles for the same reason.

One of the best ways to buy a car is to buy one that is approximately two years old from a private seller, have it thoroughly inspected by a mechanic and do not get a loan for a period longer than three years. If you cannot pay off the vehicle within three years, then you cannot afford the vehicle. I just paid off a vehicle which I purchased when it was six months old and had 6000 kilometers on it (normally I would buy an older one but the deal was too good to refuse). The vehicle cost $15,000 new, I paid $12,000 for it and paid it off within 30 months, so now I have a three-year-old car under warranty for two more years with a value of approximately $10,000 or $10,500. I have driven this car for two and a half years and it has only depreciated by about $1500. However, had I purchased this car new, it would have depreciated by about $5000.

By using the above methods you have several safeguards. Since you will be paying off the loan as fast or faster than the vehicle is depreciating, should you need to sell it you will have some money left over after you pay off your loan.

This section would not be complete without mentioning that there are substantial savings on insuring an older vehicle and it is easy to find inexpensive used parts and after-market parts.

Finally, people often do not consider the cost of maintaining a new car while it is still under warranty. One of my cars cost about $600 per year to service even though it was under warranty because of non-warranty items like brakes and tires. In the case of another car of mine, I recently phoned the dealer and was quoted $600 plus parts for the next time the car goes in for servicing. You're probably thinking it's an expensive import but in fact it is an average American car. I also called other dealers and was quoted the same price from all of them.

Managing a mortgage

A mortgage is the only form of credit that everyone should experience at some time in their life. We can do without several things, but we all need a place to live. In the long run it is much cheaper to own your own home than to rent. Unlike cars and other things people finance, real estate has always increased in value in the long term, and even if it didn't it is still a form of forced savings. Under Canadian tax laws, one of the primary reasons for investing in a private residence is that your capital gain (the increase in value from date of purchase to date of sale) is completely tax free.

However, people often get into trouble with their mortgages, mainly because their personal situation changes, i.e., the loss of one income or an increase in family size. These are situations you have some control over, but you have no control over interest rates. I have personally known people who purchased a home only to have to sell it five years later when their mortgage had to be renewed, the interest rate was double the original rate, and the payments were beyond their budget.

In general, one of the biggest misconceptions about mortgages and interest rates is that when interest rates go up two percent, for example, most people think that is no big deal, but don't be misled. I can best explain this with the following example.

■ ■ ■ ■ ■ ■ **FOR INSTANCE** ■ ■ ■ ■ ■ ■

Suppose you have a $100,000 mortgage at six percent and it is about to renew at eight percent. Most people would consider this to be a two percent increase when in fact it is a two-point increase not on 100 but on the six percent interest rate of your mortgage. It is a whopping 33 percent increase in the interest rate.

A $100,000 mortgage at six percent amortized over 25 years costs approximately $640 per month for a total of $192,000 over the life of the mortgage, $100,000 in principal plus $92,000 in interest payments.

A $100,000 mortgage at eight percent amortized over 25 years costs approximately $764 per month for a total of $229,200 over the life of the mortgage, $100,000 in principal plus $129,200 in interest payments.

Two percent of $92,000 would be $1840, but the increase is much greater. The difference between $129,200 and $92,000 is $37,200. And you can clearly see, the difference in the interest cost over the term of the mortgage is just over 40 percent.

■ ■

It may come as a surprise to know that in the first few years of a 20- or 25-year mortgage, approximately 90 percent of your mortgage payment will be going towards interest and not principal. This certainly affected the way I started to treat my mortgage. I will never forget the first year we had our mortgage and we had an option to put ten percent down on the principal at the end of every year. We had about $1000 that we considered putting down on the mortgage, but because we had been paying that all year we thought it would not make much of a difference so we spent the money on something else. About three months later we received a letter from our financial institution which broke down our total annual payments according to interest, principal, and taxes. After paying over $1000 per month for approximately nine months we had only reduced the original amount of the mortgage by $700! Ever since then I have put something on the mortgage every year.

The following table shows how much is paid off in the first five years of a $100,000 mortgage amortized over 25 years at a ten percent interest rate.

Date	Days	Payment	Interest	Principal	Balance
Year 1					
01/31	30	894.50	805.25	89.25	99910.75
02/28	31	894.50	831.48	63.02	99847.73
03/31	28	894.50	750.24	144.26	99703.47
04/30	31	894.50	829.75	64.75	99638.72
05/31	30	894.50	802.35	92.15	99546.57
06/30	31	894.50	828.44	66.06	99480.51
07/30	30	894.50	801.08	93.42	99387.09
08/31	31	894.50	827.12	67.38	99319.71
09/30	31	894.50	826.55	67.95	99251.76
10/31	30	894.50	799.24	95.26	99156.50
11/31	31	894.50	825.20	69.30	99087.20
12/31	30	894.50	797.90	96.60	98990.60
Totals		$10734.00	$9724.60	$1009.40	
Year 2					
03/31	28	894.50	742.72	151.78	98696.91
06/31	31	894.50	819.92	74.58	98448.89
09/31	31	894.50	817.82	76.68	98194.45
12/31	30	894.50	789.25	105.25	97907.27
Year 3					
06/31	31	894.50	810.76	83.74	97338.51
12/31	30	894.50	779.94	114.56	96741.23
Year 4					
06/31	31	894.50	800.43	94.07	96087.34
12/31	30	894.50	769.44	125.06	95427.31
Year 5					
06/31	31	894.50	789.04	105.46	94707.91
12/31	30	894.50	757.87	136.63	93978.72
Totals		$53670.00	$47648.13	$6021.87	

In this example the first 12 payments of $894.50 equal $10,734.00. The amount of principal paid was only $1009.40, therefore less than ten percent of your payments actually went towards principal.

Over a five-year period, 60 payments of $894.50 equal $53,670.00. The amount of principal paid was only $6021.87, which means less than 12 percent of the payments went towards the principal.

These are some of the pitfalls of having a mortgage, but there are several easier ways of paying one off. My personal favourite is to shorten the length or amortization of the mortgage by increasing the amount paid. You can take several years off your mortgage simply by marginally increasing your monthly payments. This method kept me from wasting money on less important things, and the additional money went directly towards the principal.

■ ■ ■ ■ ■ ■ **FOR INSTANCE** ■ ■ ■ ■ ■ ■

By increasing your monthly payment you can take years off your mortgage, using a $100,000 mortgage at a ten percent interest rate:

Monthly payment over 25 years = $894.50

Monthly payment over 20 years = $951.70

Monthly payment over 15 years = $1062.30

Monthly payment over 10 years = $1310.35

As you can see, by raising your payment from $894.50 to $1062.30 (only $167.80 extra per month), you would take ten years off your mortgage. If you are really aggressive you could raise your payment from $894.50 to $1310.35 (only $415.85 more), which will take 15 years off your 25-year mortgage.

The savings to you are as follows:

Total paid over 25 years = $268,350.00

Total paid over 20 years = $228,408.00

Total paid over 15 years = $191,214.00

Total paid over 10 years = $157,242.00

Wouldn't you like to save $111,108.00 on your $100,000 mortgage?

■ ■

If you are good at saving money, or you get bonuses or lump-sum payments for commission from your employer, this is a perfect opportunity to pay down your mortgage and take advantage of an annual 10 to 15 percent bulk payment allowed on most mortgages. Some institutions go by calendar year and some use the anniversary date of your individual mortgage. If you exceed the allowable bulk payment they will penalize you, so you can maximize the current year and if you have funds left over you can use them on the first day of the new year. There is usually a limit as to how many times a year you can apply a payment toward your maximum allowable bulk payment.

Another payment option being offered is the ability to double up payments on your mortgage, which will reduce your interest cost and will also allow you to miss or skip a future payment, provided you have made additional payments in the past.

A mortgage should be handled the same way as a car loan. I suggested earlier that you should pay off a car loan in three years, and the same principle should be applied to a mortgage, but over a 15-year period. Again, if you cannot pay it off in 15 years you probably cannot afford the home.

There are several options available to you today, but I would suggest you get a mortgage which allows you to increase your payments and put at least ten percent down annually. Some institutions allow you to pay weekly, which is like making a 13th payment each year. This method alone can take seven years off your mortgage.

■ ■ ■ ■ ■ ■ FOR INSTANCE ■ ■ ■ ■ ■ ■

A $100,000 mortgage at a ten percent interest rate amortized over 25 years costs $894.50 per month. Divided by four equals $224.00. If you pay $224.00 every week you are paying $224.00 × 52 (weeks) versus $894.50 × 12 (months) or an extra $894.50 per year, which will reduce your mortgage to 18 years. If you get paid every two weeks you will never even notice the extra payment. If you get paid twice per month, four months per year you will have a fifth mortgage payment.

■ ■ ■ ■ ■ ■ ■ ■ ■ ■ ■ ■ ■ ■ ■ ■ ■ ■ ■ ■

When you decide on a mortgage make certain you actually get what you requested, because some institutions will simply divide the annual amount payable by 52 and give you a weekly payment schedule. This will not reduce your amortization at all, so double-check.

Remember: you do have to repay your student loan

Student loans are managed differently now than in the past. The major banks that are handling them now are using more aggressive collection practices, so if you haven't been making your payments on your student loan, you will probably get a call from a collection agency. The Credit Bureau will be recording your missed payments, which will effect your ability to secure other credit, and Revenue Canada is also cross-checking income tax returns against student loan debt. So if you are expecting a refund but have an outstanding student loan you may not get your refund.

Statistics prove that households headed by a university graduate have a higher income and a higher standard of living. If you have a student loan and do not have a diplomã or degree then you have another problem.

If you are continuing your education or considering to further your education and require financial assistance in the form of a student loan make sure you know what courses you want and know specifically what employment opportunities will be available to you once you graduate. In a perfect world we could all go to university to educate ourselves and not consider the financial ramifications of borrowing to receive an education. However, if you are accumulating debt, six months after you graduate the financial institution will be looking to collect their money. So, only borrow what you need and take your education seriously.

I believe that in many situations a student loan is a necessity and the benefits outweigh the negatives.

Use your personal line of credit wisely

Personal lines of credit are an excellent means of financing if you only use them sporadically and for short-term situations. If you use them as an overdraft on your personal bank account, you don't have to worry about making it to the bank on payday to cover your bills. You can also use a credit line to pay off a higher interest rate debt like a credit card and then apply your payments to the credit line which would save interest costs. A credit line is like an emergency fund because it gives you access to money instantly but there are no costs if you don't use your line. I like to buy vehicles from private individuals, so if I see a good buy I can use my credit line to purchase the vehicle and then sell my existing vehicle. I may only need the credit line for a week or two to do this, and I am not without a vehicle in the interim.

Using a credit line takes discipline. There are several pitfalls of using a credit line if you don't pay it off. You can't do any of the above if you have used up all your credit. With some financial institutions you don't even have to pay any of the outstanding principal, only the interest. You may have been making minimum payments on your credit line thinking you are paying it off but you may not be at all.

Finally, the number one problem with personal lines of credit, as with credit cards, is the debt you accumulate while using them seldom leaves you with an asset that you could sell to pay off the debt.

For the Most Serious Cases

Some of you may be facing a severe financial crisis. Although my company is healthy now there was a time when my partners and I thought we'd lose everything. In this chapter I sometimes use our experience to illustrate how businesses as well as individuals can get out of debt.

Know your rights

When dealing with creditors you have the right to negotiate to have the interest on your debt waived. You can also negotiate to pay anywhere from 0 to 99 percent of the outstanding amount. I have been on both sides of this one, at different times, and as a creditor I have accepted most offers, although never the first one, because 50 percent of something is better than 100 percent of nothing.

If you and your creditor have a discrepancy in the amount of debt outstanding, ask the creditor to provide proof. This is a common stall tactic but it serves two purposes. First, it allows you to review all your charges in detail and in my experience, I have found several cases where I was overcharged. Second, by requesting a copy of your invoices, if your creditor is threatening to take you to small claims court, to collect the money your creditor will have to provide this information to the court. It is to your benefit if they have lost some of the information because you are only obligated to pay what they can prove.

There is a moral issue here if you know you owe for products or services. I have used this only for the creditors who really went beyond all limits to make things as difficult as possible for us, the ones who refused to negotiate any terms or accept any reasonable offer. Some people think that they are the only people entitled to your money. You will find some people will try and force you into bankruptcy over a couple of hundred dollars, and some to whom you owe thousands will happily negotiate balances and terms to help you get through a tough time.

Working with your creditors

If you have prepared a cash flow statement you will know how much money is available to pay off your debt, and how long it will take to pay off your creditors. Cash flow is a business term which simply means the money you expect to receive over a specific period of time offset by the anticipated expenses during the same period of time. Negotiate as much as you can and remember to prioritize the ones you must pay interest on. We did our best to negotiate terms of 6 to 12 months on debts we were paying interest on, and 12 to 24 months to pay off non-interest debt. Unfortunately, not everyone is going to want to accept your terms, especially if you are not prepared to pay interest. However, if you send several postdated cheques paying a certain amount each month, they are likely to cash them, begrudgingly accepting your terms.

The more creditors you get to accept your terms the better, for more than the obvious reasons. The big advantage of getting creditors to accept terms as quickly as possible is that it *can* actually protect you from the creditors who will not accept your terms. By doing this you are proving your attempt to repay your debt and that gives you credibility. Then if you have to show up in court, you can prove to the court that you have been repaying your debt, have made several arrangements with other creditors, and have offered terms to this creditor which were not accepted. If you have this documented and present your case properly it is unlikely that a judge will force you to pay off one creditor when it would make you default on several other previously negotiated settlements, provided the one creditor doesn't represent more than 50 percent of your debt. You will probably get the terms you are looking for and maybe even more. There is one drawback, the courts will often award interest and court costs to your creditor for the delay.

Under the Limitations Act, a debt does not have to be repaid provided you have never made a payment or acknowledged the debt in writing for a period of six years, unless your creditor has secured a judgment against you, it is collectable for ten years and can be renewed.

Don't forget to remind your creditors, or the agencies and lawyers they have representing them, that running a business or a household costs money, and you need to have some money in reserve in case of an emergency. If your car breaks down, and you need it for work or you lose your job, you must have some money to fix it. So make sure that you commit as much as possible but still have a small amount uncommitted.

When my business partner and I were sending out post-dated cheques to our creditors, we would send only six at a time just in case the unexpected happened. Well, as usual, the unexpected did happen and we tried to pay off everyone too quickly. After the six payments were made we had to go back to some of our creditors and cut the amount we were paying them by 50 percent for the balance of the debt. They were not happy about this but we did get through it all without bouncing a single cheque. I also phoned our creditors to warn them instead of just sending the smaller amount and hiding from their phone calls. It takes courage, but most people appreciate a call.

Businesses in a difficult situation should always date the cheques for the seventh or twenty-first of the month, assuming you do payroll and payables on the fifteenth and month-end. Dating them this way gives you a nice little grace period because if you commit too much, as we did, we could have had bounced cheques if payments to us in the mail did not arrive on time at month-end. Individuals may want to date cheques this way as well, just in case something happens and you cannot get to the bank on time, or you are short and need a couple days to raise the money.

Lawyers and collection agencies can be reasonable

Lawyers and collection agencies are what we fear the most when things get difficult. Having been through it I found to my surprise that these people were very helpful and easy to deal with. When you are unable to pay a creditor they may take it personally and feel as though you are trying to take advantage of them. This makes the situation very difficult when you are trying to negotiate terms or special agreements. Lawyers and collection agencies always come on strong and are threatening, but they do this because it is effective and because there are a number of people out there who just do not pay their bills, or will not pay them until they get harassed.

Everyone that these lawyers and collection agencies deal with is in some sort of financial trouble. You are no different, but you should have some kind of a plan for repaying your debt. Often they will help you put one together. You have to be honest with them but you also have to be bold and make it very clear that you have to repay all your debt and not just the creditor that they represent. When a company hires a lawyer or collection agency to collect a debt they will often accept terms based on the advice of the collector, not your advice. Your job is the same as if you were in front of a judge because in a situation like this, the collector is judge and jury, and it pays to be well prepared, so have a copy of your cash flow and a list of other creditors. Do not be afraid to let them know that you are aware of your rights, but do not make threats.

In about 60 days we had several claims placed against our company by one collection agency. I think every collector in the whole agency knew us by name. We would get a phone call per day, per claim. Finally, I called the collections manager and arranged to deal exclusively with him and to have the calls stop and to meet with him to review our situation. At our meeting I explained that we were having several problems, and that two of us were prepared to reinvest money into the company but that it was complicated by the fact that we were arranging the buyout of the other partner. This collections manager helped me to set up a cash flow and make payment arrangements. He also adjusted our interest charges and corrected improper billings.

As always, we had setbacks and were unable to make our first deadline for payments because restructuring took longer than expected. So, to avoid damaging the credibility I had previously established, I arranged for him to call our company lawyer to explain the delay and to verify what I had been telling him. This all worked out quite well and helped me deal with the other agencies who were after us. I even used him as a reference with the other agencies to make it easier to establish credibility with them and avoid harassment, so being proactive and straight forward paid off.

I also had an experience with a lawyer representing our largest creditor. I had made several offers, but they would not accept anything but payment in full, which I simply could not do. I received a call from the lawyer and returned it immediately, thanked him for calling and arranged to meet with him at his earliest convenience. At our meeting I laid my cards on the table and made him the same offer I had made the company 12 months earlier. He reviewed my material and said he would recommend my offer of payment, which involved increasing the monthly payment amount every six months, dropping the interest charges, and that the final payment be made in 24 months. It took about two weeks to get their approval, but I did get it.

If the company had accepted this offer a year before they would have already had almost half of the money owed to them and would not have had the expense of the lawyer, so be careful if you are enforcing all or nothing policies. You never know, we might have paid for a year and then gone bankrupt, but at least they would have collected some of the debt. The way they treated the situation they would have received nothing because of their lack of cooperation.

Knowing what you cannot get away with

With the previous information you are well equipped to handle the toughest collectors or lawyers. However, there are some things that you will not be able to do. You will lack credibility if you can't pay your bills, and if you try to run and hide and do not deal with the problems, you will make it more difficult to negotiate later on. Your commitment and your credibility are very important to how successfully you can negotiate terms or special deals. If you are driving a very expensive car and are not willing to sacrifice it, or you are living like a king and spending too much money, or you are not willing to reinvest some of your money into repaying your debts, why should your creditors? After all, by setting up payment terms of 3 to 24 months, you are asking them to finance you or your business. You must also realize that you can be forced into bankruptcy by your creditors if you refuse to deal with them.

Emotions do play a part here. One of our company's debtors was ordered off the stock exchange. Someone tried to resurrect the business and offered us partial payment if we waived the balance of the debt. In the past we have accepted offers like this, but this particular company's representatives had lied to us so many times and made it so difficult to get money out of them, that we decided we would not accept anything but payment in full. They tried with great persistence but we told them we would get more satisfaction knowing that they could not get back on the exchange than getting the money back. We did not get paid, but they never did recover their company. I am satisfied.

Some people think that they can hide assets and fool the courts, but the reality is that the courts have the right to trace your assets back five years and can confiscate any property or assets that you had transferred into another person's name. Any property you have used as collateral to secure financing can't be sold without approval of the financial institution, so if you sell your house to your brother on paper, and you think it is protected, think again.

Foreclosure

In very simple terms a mortgage is a contract between two or more parties whereby one party lends the necessary amount of money to the other party so they can purchase a property. The party receiving the funds pledges the property as security so, in the event they are unable to repay the debt, the other party takes over ownership of the property through the process of foreclosure.

If you are unable to make your mortgage payments and refuse to negotiate terms with the financial institution, it can legally force you into foreclosure. Most financial institutions will not start foreclosure proceedings immediately, usually only after several months of missed payments and one or more formal requests for payment.

If you are unable to make your mortgage payments on time you must contact the lender immediately and explain your situation. You should also bring a family budget showing your income and expenses because very often the lender will allow you to skip a payment or will accept a reduced payment temporarily and add the difference to your mortgage. This may be all you need to get you through a difficult time, but you won't know if you don't discuss your options with the lender. If this is unacceptable to the lender you will be forced to raise the money elsewhere or sell your home. However, they must give you a redemption period, which is usually six months.

As soon as you receive a formal request, write to or verbally contact your lawyer or, alternatively, contact legal aid or debt counselling services through Industry Canada for assistance.

It is true that for most people, their house is more than a house, it is a home. However, if you are unable to make the mortgage payments, your house loses its homey feeling very quickly. Don't hang on to old feelings and drag yourself further and further into a hole. The stress on you and your family is not worth it, and starting over is not as bad as it seems. There is no reason why you can't turn around and buy another one and make a fresh start; it may take a little while, but it will solve a major problem in your life and do wonders for your peace of mind.

Declaring bankruptcy

In 1996 there were almost 80,000 bankruptcies in Canada, approximately 50 percent more than in 1993. There are several reasons for this: unemployment, misuse of credit cards, outstanding loans, business losses, sickness, divorce, addiction, and so on.

Bankruptcy is a complicated legal process that deems you no longer responsible for your debts. Bankruptcy can complicate your life for several years, it will be recorded at the Credit Bureau and be available to virtually every credit grantor for up to six years.

Bankruptcy will stop your creditors from harassing you and will keep them from garnisheeing your wages; however, the trustee may in effect garnishee your wages anyway. Each province has its own regulations concerning the amount of personal property you can keep, some only allow you to keep as little as $2000-worth.

If you are considering bankruptcy you will require the services of a trustee. You must realize that a trustee does not work for you, in fact, they work for your creditors. There is also a minimum cost to you of approximately $1000. If the trustee feels your income is higher than you reasonably need for living expenses, they will force you to pay some of this income to your creditors.

Your bankruptcy is not complete until you receive your discharge. There are three kinds of discharge. An absolute discharge is the most common and means you are immediately no longer responsible for your debts. A suspended discharge is similar, except there is a delay before it comes into effect. A conditional discharge means you have to meet some conditions. It usually means that you pay a pre-arranged amount of money through the trustee to your creditors before you get your discharge.

Child support and alimony payments, and debts due to fraud or theft, are not eliminated by declaring bankruptcy.

Orderly payment of debt

If you find yourself in a situation where you can't pay all your debts, or at least not fast enough to keep your creditors happy, you may qualify for a plan called Orderly Payment of Debt. It is available in most, but not all, provinces at the present time. Contact Industry Canada, they are listed in "where to find additional help" at the back of this book. Find out immediately if the plan is available to you. Under the plan, a court combines your payments into one payment, excluding your mortgage, which you then send to the Debtor's Assistance Branch and they in turn pay your creditors.

All your creditors would be paid over a three- to five-year period. The plan also reduces your interest rates to five percent per year and the payments are adjusted to what you can afford. You will not have to deal with your creditors directly and they can't take legal action against you while you are on the plan. You are not permitted to borrow any more money or use your credit cards during this time.

If you have a co-signer for some of your debt, the creditor may choose to collect directly from the co-signer instead of using the plan. Creditors can also repossess secured items such as the car you bought with a car loan.

For up to six years the Credit Bureau can report the fact that you have used the program, and it will probably make it more difficult to get financing during this time. Finance companies know better than anyone that people get into financial trouble from time to time, but if they can see that you have paid off your debt they will lend again, they will want more security perhaps, but they will lend again. Orderly Payment of Debt is only available to individuals and not available to businesses.

My personal experience as a creditor and a debtor is to always be up front with your creditors and keep them up-to-date as your progress. If you call them before they call you, it puts you in a better negotiating position. By the time they call you they are likely already frustrated or angry.

If at this point you are dealing with a collections agency, by contacting them you can avoid a lot of the "strong-arm threatening approach" many collectors display and you can get down to business. Once you start to cooperate, all of this usually disappears instantly.

There Are Four Kinds of Creditors

The first and most important thing you must know when you can no longer pay your creditors is that not all creditors are the same. There are four kinds of creditors: secured, unsecured, trust or ultimately secured, and those uniquely unsecured creditors.

A secured creditor

A secured creditor is usually a financial institution that has loaned you money but has made you provide some amount of security. Any creditor who will ask for security will also charge interest and, usually, late payment penalties. A standard example is when you get a car loan. A financial institution will often only lend 75 percent of the value of the vehicle and will use the vehicle as collateral. If you default on payment they take the vehicle and sell it or auction it off to repay your loan. The same applies to a mortgage, which is secured by the equity you have in the property. If you stop paying your mortgage the financial institution will foreclose on it, which basically means they give you a fixed amount of time to raise the money or sell the home, or they do it for you.

Another form of secured credit, which usually applies to business people but can apply to individuals, is when you have to sign a personal guarantee to be granted credit for a purchase. This means that if you purchase something for your business and the business fails, you are still obligated to continue to pay for the item until it is paid in full. Usually, if they go through the trouble to get a personal guarantee they will also charge interest. If you personally extend credit to people or businesses you should implement this as part of your credit granting policy. It will not completely eliminate your bad debt but it will make a big difference. In my business, if a potential client refuses to sign a personal guarantee we will not grant them credit. We feel that if they have no confidence in their ability to pay then why should we.

An unsecured creditor

An unsecured creditor is someone who grants credit, usually in the form of products or services, but does not require you to sign a personal guarantee to secure the amount purchased with collateral. These are the people and businesses that get hurt the most when someone goes under. They have a limited number of options if a creditor refuses to pay them. They can use the services of a collection agency, the Credit Bureau, or small claims court, but unless they actually know of something you own, they cannot just show up and seize what ever they want.

Likewise, if you have leased equipment from someone else, an unsecured creditor cannot take it. If they provided you with goods or equipment they can seize that. But if you have consumed the goods they have to find something which you own free and clear of all liens and have a sheriff seize it. Now, unless you have provided this information, you can imagine how difficult it would be to recover the loss. If your business goes bankrupt or into receivership there is virtually nothing they can do to recover the money owed to them.

Receivership means the creditors of a business either appoint a receiver or get a court order to appoint a receiver, who is in charge of the liquidation of the assets of a business to pay the business's creditors. Even in receivership there is rarely enough money for the secured creditors.

Trust creditors

Trust or ultimately secured creditors apply mainly to businesses. These creditors are government agencies that rely on you to collect and remit funds on their behalf. Revenue Canada makes businesses withhold income tax, contributions to the Canada Pension Plan, Unemployment Insurance, as well as GST and PST. A provincially regulated Workers' Compensation Board may, under certain circumstances, also be a trust creditor. These creditors get paid before the banks and other secured creditors. If you are in financial difficulty this is very important. If you are considering closing down your business, and for example, you owe the bank $50,000, you may feel you have accumulated almost enough assets to cover your bank loans and that you have no other secured creditors. However, if you owe government agencies such as Revenue Canada or Workers' Compensation $40,000, they would be the first creditor paid, leaving only $10,000, so you would still owe the bank

$40,000. If you secured this loan with equity in your home or other assets, you could lose them.

Personal creditors

The last kind of creditor is of the unsecured kind, but they must be paid whether they are secured or not. These debts are usually loans from family members or suppliers that you could not survive without, and therefore they must be paid regularly.

If you are trying to protect your credit rating, as everyone should, you would have to treat your creditors equally as far as making your monthly payments is concerned. Virtually all credit grantors use the services of the Credit Bureau, which records the information that your creditors send to them about your payment habits. This information is now available to other credit grantors. So, as an example, if you stop making monthly payments on one credit card, and apply for other forms of credit, the institution you are applying to will know that you have not been making your payments. This information is available to Credit Bureau members for six years. In most cases it is unlikely that they would grant you any additional credit.

If you have never checked your credit rating you should. They are capable of making mistakes just like anyone else. If you have had trouble obtaining credit, it is possible that there is incorrect information on your credit file. You may have even thought you had corrected mistakes on your file, only to find out that they still appear. You should also know that the Credit Bureau is a private company funded by its members who, of course, have access to the credit files. I was personally shocked by this and wonder how they can resolve disputes between paying members and individuals or companies who may not have a perfect credit history.

Tips for Small Business Owners

Just a couple of ideas which helped my business partners and I pay off our debts, increase our cash flow, reduce bad debts, and improve profits.

How to improve cash flow

To improve cash flow, change the past-due aging summary on your billing from the standard aging dates of 30, 60, and 90 days to 15, 30, and 45 days. Some people only pay whatever balance is in the last column, so instead of paying at 90 days, the same people will now pay at 45 days, and you didn't even have to phone them.

Our company increased the priority on our billing to get it out faster; the faster it goes out the faster the money comes back. New businesses and businesses that have not had previous cash flow problems do not realize the importance of getting their billing out as fast as possible, and with total accuracy. If you have not analysed this area recently, take a closer look. Nothing will justify holding up payment on an invoice better than an incorrect invoice. When you are notified of an incorrect invoice, fix it immediately and send out the corrected copy. You should also request the return of the incorrect one.

There is a formula that can tell you how old a receivable is. Divide your year-to-date sales by the number of days you are into your current year; then divide your accounts receivable by this number. This is how old your receivable is in days.

■ ■ ■ ■ ■ ■ FOR INSTANCE ■ ■ ■ ■ ■ ■

There are $500,000 year-to-date sales by June 30, 182 days into the year, $100,000 in receivables, monthly sales approximately $83,000.

$$\frac{\$500,000}{182} = 2747.25$$

$$\frac{\$100,000}{2747.25} = 36.40$$

It is taking you 36.4 days to collect your money. If you bill $83,000 per month or $4150 per day you are collecting it 36.4 days later. The sooner you can collect your money the sooner you will have the $4150 in your bank instead of on your books.

■ ■ ■ ■ ■ ■ ■ ■ ■ ■ ■ ■ ■ ■ ■ ■ ■ ■ ■ ■

When we first used this formula we were well over 70 days, but have brought it down to 32 to 38 days on average. Use this formula to find out where you are now and then check it again on a monthly basis.

If you are presently billing once or twice a month, offer your clients a weekly or bimonthly billing, or put all your large clients on weekly or bimonthly billing. You probably have some good accounts that you bill at the end of every month and within one to two weeks you have already received payment. They may be paying their payables weekly, bimonthly or monthly and you could be just catching them at the right time, but most likely they are on an accounts payable cycle where they simply approve an invoice and then just issue the cheque. So, instead of waiting all month to bill them, break down their billing into a weekly rate and there is a good chance they will send payment for the first week's billing by the third week of the month. The second week's billing you would receive by the fourth week, and so on. In this situation you would have received half of their month's billings payment before you had been billing them in the past. As you can see, if they represent a large percentage of your billing, and they paid you in the same intervals, it would have a very positive effect on your cash flow.

Reducing bad debts

When we opened our business we were so anxious to get business we would take on almost any account. People used to call us and want to open an account immediately and place an order; they would say they did not have time to fill out a credit application or that they would do it later. We used to think this was great until we realized that their urgency generally meant they had been cut off by their previous supplier, and it was not long before we were cutting them off as well. Sometimes we would get paid, but often we would not. To reduce bad debts we have implemented a credit application for everyone who wants to use our service and have stopped taking accounts over the phone.

We also saw a pattern developing whereby a client's volume would all of a sudden increase. At first this would excite us, but shortly afterward they would go out of business. It was as if they knew they would not be paying for our service anyway so they would splurge, at our expense.

We also started calling for money at 30 days instead of 45 or 60 days. We would also put clients on a cash only basis at 45 days instead of 60 or longer, and we stuck to our guns. We lost some good clients by doing this, but as time went on we would hear that they had gone out of business and had burned our competitors in the progress.

In addition to asking for credit references, we now make almost everyone sign a personal guarantee as part of our credit application, as seen on the following page.

You may need to modify this slightly according to which province you live in, and you may want to have your lawyer approve it because different provinces have slightly different regulations. A collections agency is another good source for a sample guarantee and they will usually provide you with one at no charge.

Remember, when you extend credit to a client you are doing the same thing as a bank. Protect yourself and do not worry about the few clients you will lose, because if they refuse, they probably cannot afford your service anyway.

The number of small business startups is exploding these days, due to high unemployment, people becoming more specialized, and large companies not being able to afford to keep people on staff if they are really only needed for three to six months per year. Often these people contract themselves out as consultants to their previous employers. People are also trying to work from home, but when they are starting out

"In consideration of your having agreed at my request to supply ...(their company name)... with service and/or products for its business, I agree to be responsible to you for the price of all such service and/or products as you may supply to said Company and interest if applicable. This guarantee is to be an irrevocable continuing guarantee and my liability under it shall not be affected by your giving time or any other indulgence to said Company.

Dated at _____

this _____ day of _____

Witness

_____

Guarantor

_____

The above information is for the purpose of obtaining credit and is warranted to be true. I agree to pay all bills and interest if applicable, upon receipt of statement or as otherwise agreed. "

they are usually so excited to get clients that they do not get proper credit information. This can be the death of a company before it even gets started.

You may be uncomfortable asking a client to fill out a credit application and sign a guarantee; however, it probably has the opposite effect you think it has. All companies have tightened their credit-granting policies in the last several years and it has become a standard way of doing business, it even shows stability and good business sense. Companies do not like doing business with companies they can't be sure will be in business long enough to finish a contract.

When doing business always have a contract in writing and know exactly what is expected of you or your firm to avoid any disputes in the future.

Credit-reporting services offer annual premiums from approximately $250 to $2000, depending on the different needs of their clients and their budgets. They can provide monthly reports on your clients that could warn you of collection claims placed against them, or of a pattern of other suppliers not getting paid as fast as they did in the past. They can be very helpful for cash flow as well, because some of your clients will realize that the speed at which they pay you will be information available to other suppliers. Credit-reporting services can also provide past-due stickers with the name of the collection service on them. This sends a very clear message to slow-paying clients of what will happen if they do not pay their invoices.

Improving profits quickly

To improve profits, the first thing you must do is to make money with what you have. It is common for small businesses to always try to increase sales in order to increase profits. However, increased sales usually means increased expenses before it means increased profits. You have to make money today. This is the only way you can properly expand your business. An opportunity to a profitable company is usually a disaster to an unprofitable one, sinking the company further into debt.

Cutting expenses is the fastest way to improve profits in any business, but surprisingly it is not what many owners focus on. Many try to diversify into other fields, but this can be very dangerous. The first problem you will encounter by doing this is you will take on business which really is not compatible with the rest of your business or operation. You may find yourself in three or four businesses and not be very good at any of them because you are spread too thin. The second problem you will have are the increased expenses necessary to handle the diversification. Who will do the additional work? Small businesses will often try to operate without making profit for long periods, especially when starting out. This is a very dangerous pattern to get into and should be avoided. The reason you are in business is to make money, so start making some today.

We were not profitable during the time when we were dissolving our partnership, partly because we were trying to take the company in two different directions. When we finally solved this problem we were able to drastically cut expenses. We were able to instantly cut $2500 to $3000 per month over and above the wages of the partner who was no longer with us. We did not stop there either. Nothing was sacred. We scrutinized every single expense, starting with the largest and working our way down the list. If you have not gone on a cost-cutting rampage lately, you are probably way overdue. Just because you have always done things a certain way doesn't mean you must continue that way. In fact, these are the areas where you can probably save the most money. Remember: as a business your objective is to make money.

As you go through your list of expenses ask yourself these key questions.

- 💲 Why are we doing this?
- 💲 What would happen if we stopped doing this?
- 💲 Is there a more effective way of doing this?
- 💲 How can we cut some of the expense and still get the desired result?

I used to trust the so-called experts when it came to things like insurance until six years ago when I couldn't afford to renew our insurance. I found out two things: first, the only expert at saving your money is yourself; second, after investigating I found out that we could cut our premium by $4000 per year or 50 percent by self-insuring one item on our policy. We were having losses that totalled approximately $1000 per year, so even if we had insured this item there would have been a deductible of $500. By cutting this from our insurance policy our savings were about $3500 per year. I also found areas where we were under-insured and others where we were over-insured. It took about two days' work but we have saved between $16,000 and $20,000 over a five-year period and even have much better coverage. I'm not advising anyone to cancel their insurance; I'm simply stating that we had established a claims history, or track record, and based on this track record we anticipated our future losses and took the risk of self-insuring. In our case it worked out fine; it's risky but sometimes business is about taking calculated risks.

This exercise truly opened my eyes and, by interviewing several sales people and grilling them with questions as to how to maintain the best coverage with the least expense, it led to a 25 percent reduction in group insurance premiums. The sales people would all give some suggestions, and after interviewing five or six people I had a very good idea as to what we should have. The person who was so helpful with our office insurance recommended someone for our group plan who had been around for years and was an independent broker. When I met with him I didn't say anything, I just wanted to see what he could offer. He had reviewed our policy and had come up with several ways we could reduce cost and enhance coverage. I was impressed, to say the least, as with the other insurance agent providing our office insurance. One thing both of these people had in common was they were both self-employed business people with many years experience. In fact, virtually all my suppliers are reasonably small companies who are very specialized, cost effective, flexible, and certainly appreciate getting the most for your money. Usually I deal with the owners directly. There are real experts out there but you do have to go find them because they usually only operate by word-of-mouth. The best way to find them is by asking other colleagues.

I have also had substantial savings in automobile insurance, a 65 percent reduction in rent by subleasing, and several other unrelated expenses on which I would not even have considered trying to cut costs in the past.

A Taxing Problem

One tax dollar saved is two dollars earned. Average Canadians lose approximately 50 percent of their income to taxes in the form of payroll deductions, GST, PST, and taxes on property, school, luxury goods, alcohol, gasoline, cigarette tax, and on and on. Collectively, we also spend billions on permits and licences, which are also a form of taxation. You will spend more money on taxes than anything else in your lifetime, more than you will spend on your home, cars, education for your kids, or your retirement, and very likely more than everything else combined. Fortunately there are several ways to reduce taxes, including contributing to your RRSP or starting a small business in your home. Just having your loans on tax deductible items instead on non-deductible items. For example, you can reduce your taxes if you have a vehicle for work and were planning to purchase a boat. If you only need to finance one of them, you should pay cash for the boat and finance the vehicle because you can deduct some of the interest.

This book is not a tax planning guide, but it is impossible to write about finances without mentioning taxes. Proper money management has to include a tax planning component so you can be certain you are not wasting your hard-earned money on overpaying your taxes. Every year there are a number of inexpensive income tax guides. I strongly suggest you read one of these books because you could learn how to save thousands of dollars annually.

If you use accountants and leave everything up to them you must understand that it is very difficult for them to know everything about your personal circumstances. If you're like most people you show up at their busiest time of year and are probably in a hurry yourself. The better prepared you are the better the job your accountant can do for you. The best time to see your accountant is well before or after tax time, when they are not so busy.

Setting Financial Goals

Most people hate to be told to set goals for themselves. I was no different even though I had purchased a house before many of my friends had finished university and had started a business when I was 25. I still did not take goal setting very seriously, it was more or less just an exercise, like making New Year's resolutions. Six years ago I started writing down my goals in all areas of my life. I put them in a book and reviewed them every six months to stay focused, and added new ones. I did this for about three years, always looking forward and never looking back. One day I found that first book and started reading about what was so important to me at that time, and the goals I had set. It was amazing what I had achieved over three years off those lists. I had quit smoking, lost weight, taken up new sports, bought new cars and houses, started a family, was better educated, and on and on. You may attribute this to maturity, but I had also surpassed every financial goal I had set three years earlier. I take goal setting much more seriously now.

You should refer back to your personal balance sheet and debt worksheet to help you set some short-term financial goals, but you will have to use your imagination for your long-term goals. Set short-term and long-term goals from three to six months then one, three, five, and ten years. Write them down and also write down why it is important to you to achieve them. Don't forget about them, make a copy and tape it to your refrigerator or bathroom mirror where you can see it regularly. Someone once said goals are just dreams with a deadline.

The following page is a goal-setting worksheet which covers short-term goals and long-term goals. Take some time to consider where you want to go in your life. You don't even need to know how you are going to get there, just write down your goals and review them regularly and you will find that ideas and opportunities will come to you.

An obvious goal would be to get out of debt. How about setting a goal to be a lender instead of a borrower, so instead of paying interest you are collecting interest?

■ ■

GOAL-SETTING WORKSHEET

3-6-month Goals

_____

_____

_____

_____

_____

_____

_____

_____

1-Year Goals

_____

_____

_____

_____

_____

_____

_____

_____

3-Year Goals

_____

_____

_____

_____

_____

_____

_____

_____

5-Year Goals

_____

_____

_____

_____

_____

_____

_____

_____

10-Year Goals

_____

_____

_____

_____

_____

_____

_____

_____

■ ■

Where to Find Additional Help

Originally I had a list of local phone numbers for each province, but while I was verifying them just before publishing most of them had changed. I suspect this is mostly due to changes in governments. There is not a federal program for individuals, only provincial programs, which are not necessarily provincial government offices, sometimes they are just funded by the provincial government. Industry Canada, even though it is part of the federal government, is probably the quickest way to get a local phone number, and you can call for credit counselling services. Their location is given in your local directory. You could also contact your provincial government reference or information numbers in your local directory and ask for debt counselling services or credit couunselling services. These services are usually free of charge.

For small business owners you may want to contact the Business Development Bank of Canada (BDC) formerly Federal Business Development Bank (FBDB), which operates all across Canada and provides access to business owners at a fraction of the cost of private consultants. The BDC offers the service of several semi-retired business people from different industries who I'm certain could earn substantially more money in private consulting but are willing to help out other business owners. You will have to spend some money but you will get very good advice and your own counsellor for much less than private sector rates. I have personally used these services when my business was in trouble and I highly recommend them. They also offer seminars and workshops covering all areas of business and financial management. There are 84 BDC offices across Canada, for the phone number and location of the branch closest to you call toll free 1-888-INFO BDC, 1-888-463-6232, or check your local phone book.

You can also contact any of the bankruptcy trustees listed in your local yellow pages. You don't have to be considering bankruptcy to get their assistance with debt counselling.

Laws vary from region to region and policies keep changing, so if you are in default and are getting calls from creditors, seek the advice of a credit counsellor so you are sure you know all your options.

Keeping the Money Flowing

In order to achieve your financial goals you have to keep the money flowing. It's very difficult trying to keep up with your bills if you aren't working, and it is a lot easier to pay them if you can increase your income. I discussed increasing your income in an earlier chapter but it was mainly for short-term situations. In this chapter, I want to go into more depth to give you some ideas, which if you follow them, will help you increase your earning potential for years to come.

Eleven years owning and managing a business, hiring and training and firing employees has, I feel, given me an opportunity to share some thoughts of how you can get a job, get a raise or promotion, and always be in demand.

Walk in and ask for a job

First, to get a job, simply just go get one. I managed a growing business for seven or eight years, constantly hiring people on a weekly basis without placing an advertisement in a newspaper. I would just put up a sign in front of the office.

If you never came by you would never have a chance of being hired. I know several business people who hire people without advertising. They hire through word-of-mouth, and take on people who just come in and apply for positions, even when the company isn't hiring. My partner and I have hired people when we had no intention of hiring: these people came to us and convinced us we could use their services.

Where do you want to be?

Decide what type of work you want to do. If this is difficult for you, as it is with many people, you may just be looking in the wrong places, or thinking of work as work. Work can be fun, and it is fun for many successful people, because they pursue careers in areas that they enjoy. What are your hobbies? Do you have a small or part-time business that you do for fun? What if your hobbies became your business? Wouldn't that be enjoyable? If you dream of owning a business one day, what type of business would it be? If you know the answer to this, are you working in a related field? If not, you are working away from your goals instead of toward them. Work for a company in the industry you want to be in and learn as much as possible about the business. This will confirm your commitment to the industry and provide the knowledge and contacts in the industry which you will need in the future.

How to get there

Once you know what you want to do, find out every possible employer who could use your services. Try to determine which companies are growing. The faster-growing the company, the more likely they are to be hiring, or will be hiring in the near future, and also the better your chances for advancement within the company. Send them a resumé, follow up with a visit, follow that up with a phone call. Perhaps you would consider an entry-level position with the right company. This would give you the chance to learn their business, which would give you a better opportunity to advance when the position you want comes available. I, like many business people, keep a file of resumés that people send to me. When I need to fill a position, it's the first place I look. Business people look very favourably on people who are out there trying to make things happen. And they know you can't have too many people who make things happen.

When applying for work you must make your first impression the best possible. This will likely be your only chance to make a good impression, because if you don't, you probably won't get a second opportunity. Some of the worst first impressions I have experienced while interviewing are: people who arrive late; not at all, but call; come in unshaven and dirty; smoking, in a non-smoking office; swearing, drunk, etc. Don't do any of the above. Dress appropriately and conduct yourself suitably for the position you are applying for.

Work, Commitment, and Adaptability

The best way to get a raise or promotion is always to do more than is asked of you. Willingness to work and commitment are more important in many businesses than education or experience. Most jobs are being created by small specialized businesses that provide a lot of on-the-job training. The success of these businesses is their ability to adapt and to change to suit their customers' need for change. For your personal success you have to be willing to accept change, because with change comes opportunity. If your company is installing new technology, be the first to volunteer. The more you learn about it, the more opportunity you will have to teach others, and the more important you will become to your company. Other employees, who refuse to learn new technology, will most likely be replaced by the technology, or will be replaced with people who are willing to work with it. I personally experienced this in my own company when we changed to a fully computerized company. The majority of the staff resisted change, and even though we provided training and encouragement, and even incentives, within six months we had to replace most of the staff. The new people were thriving in the same environment that the others just couldn't deal with. Out of approximately twelve staff only four were willing to learn the technology, and wouldn't you know it, those four people became the highest paid in our company, and had steady employment for as long as they chose to stay. Two of them remained for over ten years, and even stayed on with the company after it was sold to new owners. One is still with the company and the other decided to change careers and left on his own terms about a year ago.

The lesson here is simple. Employers can teach skills to people who are willing to learn, accept change and are committed, but they can't teach willingness, adaptability, and commitment to anyone.

Treat your current job as if it were your dream job. Some people don't take their jobs seriously, they show up late, book off time, and have a bad attitude. When they get the opportunity they have been waiting for, they often blow it because they have brought with them all their bad habits, and they end up losing their dream job. So start practising good habits now so you will have them when the opportunity arrives for a better position.

Staying may be better than switching

Being patient and staying with the right company is sometimes much better than jumping around from company to company. I have had employees who jump from job to job. Then they end up on my doorstep and want me to hire them back. They may have had four jobs in three years. As an employer I can't expect to keep this person for very long, so why should I spend time and money training them? Had they stayed with one company they probably would have advanced in the company or at least would have earned more money and had some stability. People who change jobs often miss out on opportunities because just as they start becoming valuable to their company they leave.

If you want a raise, or a promotion, do some self-analysis and ask yourself the following questions...

- ⑤ What did I do today?
- ⑤ Did I earn my pay?
- ⑤ What was it worth to my company?
- ⑤ If you owned the company, would you hire you?
- ⑤ Would you fire you?
- ⑤ Give you a raise or promotion?
- ⑤ Why?
- ⑤ What can you do to be worth more to your company?
- ⑤ Have you ever asked your boss this question? If you haven't, you should.
- ⑤ Can you do your job more efficiently, allowing you to take on more responsibility?

With all the news about mergers and downsizing, many people feel jaded and wonder if their efforts are being noticed. I can sympathize with these people and understand their frustration; however, it is important to be positive and stay focused, because even in a merger or downsizing situation the executives are displaced as well. You can be sure they are out there looking for new opportunities and they often take staff with them. Any executive, worth his or her pay, given the opportunity to make a change of companies, or start up a new division in a company, would know, without hesitation, to whom they would offer positions in the new company. Also, any executive who is given a mandate to reduce 10 or 20 percent of their staff could probably make this decision very easily. So even if your current employer is not recognizing your contributions (and perhaps for financial reasons they can't), other people will. If you're a top producer in your company, your competition will know who you are. They have probably offered you a position in their company. Top producers in any field are never without opportunity.

We will never be able to stop technology from replacing people, and let's face it, we love it, until technology replaces us. Payroll taxes and labour costs are forcing business to utilize technology wherever possible. As workers this frustrates us, but as consumers we want to have the cost savings and flexibility. For example, being able to go to the bank at ten o'clock on a Sunday night, and do all our banking and pay our bills. We certainly wouldn't want to stand in line waiting for a teller; and imagine the service fees we would have if banks offered tellers 24 hours a day, 7 days a week.

You must remember who you really work for. You are "YOU INC." and you work for yourself. Everyone is truly self-employed, all any of us really do is trade our services for money. Before the industrial revolution work was training, a form of apprenticeship so you could learn a skill and then you would eventually start your own business. Once you were established and busy enough you would teach your children or take on an apprentice of your own. The ideal of leaving school, getting a job, working for 30 years for the same company and retiring with your gold watch is really a very short-lived phenomenon which has already passed. You will likely change jobs several times during your career. I am only in my mid-thirties and I have two careers, my third and fourth. I am sure I will have more. Protect yourself, and increase your worth by learning new skills and new technologies. All of the community colleges offer evening and weekend courses so you can upgrade your skills. Many companies will pay for employee-training courses. If you haven't been to your local library lately you should stop by. Libraries are full of books covering every area of personal growth, business, computers, software, etc. Virtually any skill you want to acquire, you can find information on it at your library. They even have videos on all the different computer software programs; you can watch them in 90 minutes and pickup shortcuts,and new skills which could make you more efficient at your job instantly. Motivational tapes are great to listen to as well because they allow you to dream, and at the same time encourage you to stay focused on your goals. In an earlier chapter I wrote **Fail to Plan, Plan to Fail**. It's time to set a plan for your career. Just as with your financial goals, I want you to set career goals for three to six months, then one, three, five, and ten years.

It is time to make changes. Remember: the only thing consistent in life is change. Don't be afraid of change, welcome it, and prepare yourself to take advantage of the opportunities it provides. We can all achieve so much more if we just commit ourselves. We are surrounded by opportunities everywhere. If you aspire to own your own business, you will have to do all of the above, so why not start practising it now?

Conclusion

If you're broke, you're in good company. Many successful people and businesses have experienced severe financial problems. Don't be too hard on yourself, no one plans to go broke, it just seems to happen, usually because of a lack of knowledge or inexperience. You now have the knowledge to get back on more stable ground, and if you use this knowledge you will have seen the worst of your problems. Promise yourself that you will follow through and get your financial house in order. Work on developing better habits and be more effective with your money. You don't have to change your life, just your spending habits. Get creative, there is always a way, and you don't need to commit to these ideas for life, it's only a temporary measure while you regroup. It may appear to take a long time, but once you get started you will be amazed at the difference a couple of years can make. I thought it would take me forever, but within two years I was better off than I thought I would be before I got into trouble. I am certain you will eventually look back on the hard times and say the same thing. This book is another good thing which came out of my situation and I hope it will make a difference to your financial success.

Finally, saving the best for the last, once you commit to my advice, and make the necessary sacrifices to tame your personal debt, you will experience a very different feeling than you would expect. You will not experience a feeling of sacrifice, you will experience the feelings of being in control of your finances, and taking charge of your life.

■
Budget Worksheets

■ ■

WEEKLY HOUSEHOLD BUDGET
(Handy Shopping List)

Fruit

_____	$_____
_____	$_____
_____	$_____
_____	$_____

Vegetables

_____	$_____
_____	$_____
_____	$_____
_____	$_____

Meat

_____	$_____
_____	$_____
_____	$_____
_____	$_____

Milk/Milk Products (cheese, butter, etc.)

_____	$_____
_____	$_____
_____	$_____
_____	$_____
_____	$_____
_____	$_____
_____	$_____
_____	$_____

Margerine, Oils (vegetable, olive, etc.)

_____	$_____
_____	$_____
_____	$_____
_____	$_____

Eggs

_____	$_____

Subtotal $_____

Breads

_____	$_____
_____	$_____
_____	$_____
_____	$_____

Cereals

_____	$_____
_____	$_____
_____	$_____

Pastas/Rice/Beans

_____	$_____
_____	$_____
_____	$_____
_____	$_____

Coffee/Tea

_____	$_____
_____	$_____

Baking Products (flour, mixes, etc.)

_____	$_____
_____	$_____
_____	$_____
_____	$_____

Juice/Pop

_____	$_____
_____	$_____
_____	$_____
_____	$_____

Canned Goods

_____	$_____
_____	$_____
_____	$_____
_____	$_____
_____	$_____

Subtotal $_____

Frozen Foods

_____ $_____

_____ $_____

_____ $_____

_____ $_____

Condiments

_____ $_____

_____ $_____

_____ $_____

_____ $_____

_____ $_____

Cookies/Snack Foods

_____ $_____

_____ $_____

_____ $_____

_____ $_____

Pet Food

_____ $_____

_____ $_____

Sundries

_____ $_____

_____ $_____

_____ $_____

_____ $_____

Cleaning Products

_____ $_____

_____ $_____

_____ $_____

_____ $_____

Paper Products

_____ $_____

_____ $_____

_____ $_____

Subtotal $_____

Drycleaning

_____ $_____

Office/School Supplies

_____ $_____

_____ $_____

_____ $_____

_____ $_____

Car (Gas, Oil, Parking, etc.)

_____ $_____

_____ $_____

_____ $_____

_____ $_____

Miscellaneous Household (indoors, outdoors)

_____ $_____

_____ $_____

_____ $_____

_____ $_____

Other

_____ $_____

_____ $_____

_____ $_____

_____ $_____

Weekly Treats

_____ $_____

_____ $_____

_____ $_____

Total $_____

■ ■

■ ■

FAMILY NEEDS
(clothing, school, sports, music lessons, etc.)

Item	Date Needed	Amount Saved	Total Cost
1.		$	$
2.		$	$
3.		$	$
4.		$	$
5.		$	$
6.		$	$
7.		$	$
8.		$	$
9.		$	$
10.		$	$
11.		$	$
12.		$	$
13.		$	$
14.		$	$
15.		$	$
16.		$	$
17.		$	$
18.		$	$
19.		$	$
20.		$	$

■ ■

Index